Brown University
Providence, Rhode Island

Written by Matthew R. Kittay

Edited by Adam Burns, Kimberly Moore, and Jaime Myers

Layout by Jon Skindzier

Additional contributions by Omid Gohari, Christina Koshzow, Chris Mason, Joey Rahimi, and Luke Skurman

ISBN # 1-4274-0028-8
ISSN # 1551-9635

Last updated 5/11/06

Special Thanks To: Babs Carryer, Andy Hannah, LaunchCyte, Tim O'Brien, Bob Sehlinger, Thomas Emerson, Andrew Skurman, Barbara Skurman, Bert Mann, Dave Lehman, Daniel Fayock, Chris Babyak, The Donald H. Jones Center for Entrepreneurship, Terry Slease, Jerry McGinnis, Bill Ecenberger, Idie McGinty, Kyle Russell, Jacque Zaremba, Larry Winderbaum, Roland Allen, Jon Reider, Team Evankovich, Lauren Varacalli, Abu Noaman, Mark Exler, Daniel Steinmeyer, Jared Cohon, Gabriela Oates, David Koegler, and Glen Meakem.

Bounce-Back Team: Brian Nagendra, Ben Goetsch, and Emily Kanstroom

College Prowler®
5001 Baum Blvd.
Suite 750
Pittsburgh, PA 15213

Phone: 1-800-290-2682
Fax: 1-800-772-4972
E-Mail: info@collegeprowler.com
Web Site: www.collegeprowler.com

Welcome to College Prowler®

During the writing of College Prowler's guidebooks, we felt it was critical that our content was unbiased and unaffiliated with any college or university. We think it's important that our readers get honest information and a realistic impression of the student opinions on any campus—that's why if any aspect of a particular school is terrible, we (unlike a campus brochure) intend to publish it. While we do keep an eye out for the occasional extremist—the cheerleader or the cynic—we take pride in letting the students tell it like it is. We strive to create a book that's as representative as possible of each particular campus. Our books cover both the good and the bad, and whether the survey responses point to recurring trends or a variation in opinion, these sentiments are directly and proportionally expressed through our guides.

College Prowler guidebooks are in the hands of students throughout the entire process of their creation. Because you can't make student-written guides without the students, we have students at each campus who help write, randomly survey their peers, edit, layout, and perform accuracy checks on every book that we publish. From the very beginning, student writers gather the most up-to-date stats, facts, and inside information on their colleges. They fill each section with student quotes and summarize the findings in editorial reviews. In addition, each school receives a collection of letter grades (A through F) that reflect student opinion and help to represent contentment, prominence, or satisfaction for each of our 20 specific categories. Just as in grade school, the higher the mark the more content, more prominent, or more satisfied the students are with the particular category.

Once a book is written, additional students serve as editors and check for accuracy even more extensively. Our bounce-back team—a group of randomly selected students who have no involvement with the project—are asked to read over the material in order to help ensure that the book accurately expresses every aspect of the university and its students. This same process is applied to the 200-plus schools College Prowler currently covers. Each book is the result of endless student contributions, hundreds of pages of research and writing, and countless hours of hard work. All of this has led to the creation of a student information network that stretches across the nation to every school that we cover. It's no easy accomplishment, but it's the reason that our guides are such a great resource.

When reading our books and looking at our grades, keep in mind that every college is different and that the students who make up each school are not uniform—as a result, it is important to assess schools on a case-by-case basis. Because it's impossible to summarize an entire school with a single number or description, each book provides a dialogue, not a decision, that's made up of 20 different topics and hundreds of student quotes. In the end, we hope that this guide will serve as a valuable tool in your college selection process. Enjoy!

OMID GOHARI ○ CHRISTINA KOSHZOW ○ CHRIS MASON ○ JOEY RAHIMI ○ LUKE SKURMAN ○
The College Prowler Team

Table of Contents

Introduction from the Author

When I began to look at colleges in my junior year of high school, I knew very little about the specific schools of the Northeast. Being from Tampa, Florida, large Northeast schools were something few of my classmates were considering and even fewer applied to. I knew the big cities were New York and Boston, so I started my search there. After a few months, one of my teachers, a Brown alumnus, suggested that I should check out Brown University in Providence, Rhode Island. Although I knew Brown was an Ivy League school, and was supposed to be academically impressive, I knew very little about the school and even less about Providence. But now, after four years here, I have become an expert on Brown and Providence.

As you head toward Brown on Interstate 95, first you may be struck by the quaint New England factory towns, and then Providence's downtown emerges from the horizon. Getting lost in the maze of local one-way streets lined with historic houses and buildings is all part of the Providence experience. Providence's self-proclaimed "Renaissance" features fresh paint and smooth roads that clash with winter torn streets and century-old houses that make up the historic east side neighborhoods around Brown.

Once you are on campus, you will see students swarming along the greens, the streets, and the sidewalks even on the bitterest days, rushing in and out of the Rockefeller Library until 2 a.m. Most people should be able to point you towards the admissions building, only two blocks away from the Rock, and will chat with you once you ask them for directions. Go on the tour first so you don't miss anything wandering around by yourself, but do yourself a favor and don't fully base your opinion of Brown on a one-hour rehearsed speech.

While the tour gives a digest of the University layout, you don't really get to meet the students. If you really want to know the school, meet the students. That's why I've written this book. Being a Brown student myself, my voice in this edition will help you know at least one Brown student's view. In addition, and more importantly, the hours of transcribed interviews let you know what life on campus is really like. It will give you insight into how Brown students feel when it comes to the issues that most concern them. This book will give prospective students a sense for the school without ever stepping foot on campus. Also, if you come to visit Brown, it will help you get the most out of your trip.

Good luck and enjoy the read.

Matthew Kittay, Author
Brown University

By the Numbers

General Information

Brown University
45 Prospect St.
Providence, RI 02912

Control:
Private

Academic Calendar:
Semester system

Founded:
1764

Web Site:
www.brown.edu

Main Phone:
(401) 863-1000

Admissions Phone:
(401) 863-2378

Student Body

**Full-Time
Undergraduates:**
5,708

**Part-Time
Undergraduates:**
306

**Full-Time Male
Undergraduates:**
2,740

**Full-Time Female
Undergraduates:**
3,274

Admissions

Overall Acceptance Rate:
17%

Early Decision Acceptance Rate:
29%

Regular Acceptance Rate:
15%

Total Applicants:
15,286

Total Acceptances:
2,534

Freshmen Enrollment:
1,458

Yield (% of admitted students who actually enroll):
58%

Early Decision Available?
Yes

Early Action Available?
No

Total Early Decision Applicants:
1,863

Total Early Decision Acceptances:
27%

Early Decision Deadline:
November 1

Early Decision Notification:
Mid-December

Regular Decision Deadline:
January 1

Regular Decision Notification:
First week in April

Must-Reply-By Date:
May 1

Applicants Placed on Waiting List:
1,400

Applicants Accepted from Waiting List:
450

Applicants Enrolled from Waiting List:
89

Transfer Applications Received:
686

Transfer Applications Accepted:
189

Transfer Students Enrolled:
108

Transfer Student Acceptance Rate:
28%

Common Application Accepted?
No

Supplemental Forms?
No

Admissions E-Mail:
admissions_undergrad@
brown.edu

➜

Admissions Web Site:
www.brown.edu/
administration/Admission

SAT I or ACT Required?
Either

First-Year Students Submitting SAT Scores:
96%

SAT I Range (25th–75th Percentile):
1310–1520

SAT I Verbal Range (25th–75th Percentile):
650–760

SAT I Math Range (25th–75th Percentile):
660–760

SAT II Requirements:
Any 3 SAT IIs

Retention Rate:
97%

Top 10% of High School Class:
90%

Application Fee:
$70

Financial Information

Full-Time Tuition:
$32,974

Room and Board:
$8,796

Books and Supplies:
$1,096

Average Need-Based Financial Aid Package (including loans, work-study, grants, and other sources):
$24,402

Students Who Applied For Financial Aid:
51%

Students Who Received Aid:
45%

Financial Aid Forms Deadline:
November 1 (Early Decision)
February 1 (Regular Admission)

Financial Aid Phone:
(401) 863-9922

Financial Aid E-Mail:
FinAid_Administrator@brown.
edu

Financial Aid Web Site:
http://financialaid.brown.edu

Academics

The Lowdown On...
Academics

Degrees Awarded:
Bachelor of Arts
Bachelor of Science
Master
First Professional
Doctorate

Most Popular Majors:
8% History
7% International relations
6% Biology
6% Political science
5% Psychology

Undergraduate Schools:
Brown College

Full-Time Faculty:
762

Faculty with Terminal Degree:
96%

Student-to-Faculty Ratio:

8:1

Graduation Rates:
Four-year: 83%
Five-year: 94%
Six-year: 96%

Average Course Load:

4 courses

Special Degree Options

Brown's Program in Liberal Medical Education (PLME) is an eight-year program combining a liberal arts education with medical school. Freshmen are accepted to the college and medical school as freshmen and spend eight years at Brown completing their BA and MD.

Brown also offers master's degrees in some departments for undergraduates who add on an additional year of study.

AP Test Score Requirements

Students might receive credit for scores of 4 or 5, but check the Brown Web site for a complete list of accepted tests and scores. Typically, high AP test scores will get you placement in advanced classes but not course credit.

Best Places to Study

The John D. Rockefeller Library (the Rock) or the Sciences Library (the Sci-Li), the Blue Room, coffee shops on Thayer Street, dorm computer clusters, and study rooms.

Sample Academic Clubs

African Students Association, Asian American Student Association, Bio-medical Engineering Society, Brown Film Society, Chinese Student Association, Engineering Society, Pre-Med Chapter AMSA, Women Students at Brown, Shakespeare on the Green

Did You Know?

Brown does not have any general course requirements. While you must complete a total of 30 courses and specific courses within a concentration (Brown's word for major), there are **absolutely no course requirements**. You'll never have to take another math or English class if you don't want to. This system, known as the New Curriculum, started in 1969.

In line with this educational philosophy, most classes at Brown can be taken with a grade option of **A/B/C/No Credit or Satisfactory/No Credit**.

If one of Brown's hundreds of concentrations doesn't appeal to you, you can **make up your own**. An independent concentration is a course of study designed by the student with the guidance of University professors and deans that combines classes from different concentrations to show relations and connections between different studies.

Students Speak Out On...
Academics

"A lot of classes I have taken in my first two years have been taught by graduate students. You have to take initiative and go to office hours to get to know your professors."

"Because **there is no core curriculum**, you aren't typically forced into any bad courses. The skills and styles of teachers at Brown vary widely—as they probably do everywhere. But Brown does tell you to judge for yourself. The first several weeks of every semester is a 'shopping period' during which you can try out as many classes as you can pack into your day. Not everyone shops around, but most students shop at least a little. Shopping can be extremely useful for weeding out the incoherent mumblers and the digressive babblers, and for hunting down the best teachers."

"Almost every semester I have taken at least one course that has had a profound impact on my life. These classes have ranged from Early Modern Philosophy, Intro to Object Oriented Programming, and Seminar in the Teaching of Writing to Intro to Neuroscience. **I have taken some courses that I misjudged** while scheduling classes, but I think that's part of the learning experience, too, to learn to craft your own education."

Q "I get to switch it up a little bit. I think the Brown curriculum offers a lot of space to try things out and really figure out what you are interested in. I transferred for the open curriculum. I think when people first start applying to the school, they don't realize or pay attention to how much the curriculum of the school and the educational philosophy can influence your experience at a place. **My other school was way too restrictive**."

Q "**I didn't get a chance to develop close relationships with my professors** freshman year, because I took a lot of big intro classes. I did take one class where the professor led the sections and really got to know the students by taking pictures of all the students and putting our names on them, so when he called on someone, he knew who it was. It was a smaller class, but I felt like I got to know him that way."

Q "It took me a long time to figure out what I really wanted to concentrate in because **Brown really lets you explore whatever you want** when you get here. I wouldn't say that's a bad thing. I decided on visual arts, and I'm really happy about that. I knew I didn't want to go to an art school because I wanted to take more academic classes and have more of a background for my work, and that's exactly what Brown allowed me to do. I made my own experience out of it."

Q "The **teachers are a mixed bag**. Most all of them are on the very high end of the intelligence scale. However, some are very interested in students and teaching, while others seem to care less as they write their grants or just appear lazy when it comes to making interesting lesson plans and assignments. Most I ended up liking and learning from."

Q "My experiences with graduate students as teachers have been really good. Freshman year, I took a philosophy class and the material was really good, but **the professor was horrible**. It was one of the few classes I've taken where a TA was in charge of teaching in a section, not just reviewing the material, and the TA was so much better than the professor."

Q "My teachers have been great. Because of the open curriculum, I think **teachers know that you are choosing to be in their class, so they are pretty excited to have you there**, and they tend to go the extra mile and help you if you need it with things like setting work up for the summer. I've had really good experiences. I took a sociology class my first year and the professor had just come over here a year or two before that. We met almost every week—I helped her with English, and she taught me the readings. It was really cool."

Q "People often develop quirky relationships with their professors. Now I'm doing research with a professor whose class I was in last semester. **I've had some great teachers** and some great graduate students."

Q "I took a lecture and a seminar with my thesis advisor. At first, after the lecture, **our relationship was distant**. In the seminar, however, we had in-depth discussions and had dinner at the professor's house with a guest lecturer from the class, who was a big policy maker in his field."

Q "Brown has the best neuroscience department. The **professors are on top and leading the field**. They teach from the best books in the field, which are also written here by the department."

Q "Many of my classes were interesting. Sometimes when taking many courses in the same department, **I found that they were a bit repetitive**. I had a few that were incredible, and a few that were miserable, but overall, the course selection and courses themselves at Brown are great."

Q "**Brown has a cross curriculum with the Rhode Island School of Design**; you can take up to four courses there for Brown credit."

Q "I can go to lectures and classes at RISD. As a visual art major, that's a big plus. **Access to RISD is very useful, but it's definitely not easy**. Scheduling and getting into classes can be complicated. But if you are persistent, there are tons of resources. You have to make it a priority."

Q "I think Brown is a place where people have a couple really good, **personal experiences with professors**. You go to their office hours or out for a drink and really spend a lot of time together. That's balanced with your lecture courses, where you go or you don't go. But that's what's good about it, since there is not a graduate program in a lot of departments."

The College Prowler Take On...
Academics

At Brown, persistence and personal responsibility play a big role in defining the undergraduate career. Students are rewarded for learning to work within Brown's small and intimate academic departments. In other words, it is always possible to work the system. Students always have a good chance of getting into high-level classes even if they are outside their concentration. Many students come to Brown uncertain of their concentrations, and many switch their concentrations more than once in their undergraduate career. Brown's academic philosophy encourages exploration into new areas of study which can spark new interests or projects. In general, Brown believes that every student knows what's best for him or herself.

Unlike other elite universities, Brown's primary focus is on undergraduate students. In accordance with this goal, all Brown professors are required to teach an undergraduate class which gives students access to some of the top academics in their field. Most students are able to make strong connections with at least a few professors who provide them with support as they develop their own interests. There are, of course, shortcomings to Brown's system. The lack of many professional schools, like law or a business schools, can make the post-Brown transition a bit jarring. In addition, for a large university, Brown can sometimes seem to have a limited number of courses available, with some departments lacking a large enough staff to support all the students. Often, you have to try for several semesters to get into a popular or limited-enrollment class. However, with persistence, anything is possible at Brown.

The College Prowler® Grade on
Academics: A

A high Academics grade generally indicates that professors are knowledgeable, accessible, and genuinely interested in their students' welfare. Other determining factors include class size, how well professors communicate, and whether or not classes are engaging.

Local Atmosphere

The Lowdown On...
Local Atmosphere

Region:
Northeast

City, State:
Providence, RI

Setting:
Urban

Distance from Boston:
1 hour

**Distance from
New York City:**
4 hours

Points of Interest:

India Point Park

Lupo's at the Strand

Newport Beaches

Outdoor Ice Rink at
Kennedy Plaza

Purgatory Chasm

The RISD Museum

Roger Williams Park Zoo

Waterplace Park

→

Closest Movie Theaters:

Avon Cinema
260 Thayer St.
Providence
(401) 421-3315

The Cable Car Cinema
204 South Main St.
Providence
(401) 272-3970

The Castle Cinema
1039 Chalkstone Ave.
Providence
(401) 751-3456

Closest Shopping Areas:

Providence Place Mall, Wayland Square, Wickenden Street, and Thayer Street.

College favorites like Wal-Mart and Sam's Club are also just a short car ride away.

Major Sports Teams:

New England Patriots (football)

Boston Red Sox (baseball)

City Web Sites

www.providenceri.com

www.brown.dailyjolt.com

www.oso.com

Did You Know?

5 Fun Facts about Brown:

- Providence hosts Waterfire on weekend nights in late spring, summer, and early fall. Ninety-seven bonfires line the river at Waterplace Park. Local residents enjoy the fires, music, and food vendors as they walk along the river. Artist Barnaby Evans, a Brown graduate, created Waterfire for the city's newly renovated riverside area in 1994.

- A few times a semester RISD, hosts a student art sale on Benefit Street. There's no better place to buy your holiday or birthday presents.

- Brown is about a 10-minute walk from the world-famous Lupo's Heartbreak Hotel, where big and small shows, from punk to jazz, happen on an almost nightly basis.

- Once a month, Providence, hosts Gallery Night. Galleries around the city, including Brown's Bell Gallery, open their doors and wine cellars to locals who want to take in a little culture. Brown and RISD student art is almost always part of the event.

- Recently, Providence has been the stage for numerous movies and TV shows. The obvious examples are the film *Outside Providence* and the show *Providence* on that was on NBC. Perhaps the most accurate portrayal of Providence is in *Family Guy*, which was written by a RISD graduate.

Local Slang:

Bubbler – a water fountain

Coffee Milk – like chocolate milk, but with coffee syrup

College Hill – the hill in Providence where Brown and RISD are located

Dropped Egg – a poached egg East Side – the gentrified side of Providence where Brown is located

Extra, Extra – extra cream, extra sugar at Dunkin' Donuts

Light and Sweet – coffee with cream and sugar at Rhode Island staple Dunkin' Donuts

Projo – the *Providence Journal*

Quahog – a big clam

Roe Dylin – how the locals say where they're from

Stuffies – a stuffed quahog

Famous Rhode Islanders:

Harry Anderson, the Farrelly Brothers, Emeril Lagasse, H.P. Lovecraft, and Samuel Slater

Students Speak Out On...
Local Atmosphere

{ **"The mall is right here. You really need to get off campus sometimes, but you don't have to go that far; downtown is great."**

Q "I love Thayer Street. **There's so much to it**. I've never been anywhere quite like it."

Q "Providence is what you make of it. **The town has a lot to offer**—from parks to hang out in, to bars, clubs, and restaurants. Other universities are present, but aside from RISD, there is little interaction between Brown students and other area university students. Check out the Waterfire and the mall on rainy days!"

Q "**Providence is an ideal city for college**. The city is easily navigable, not overpowering, and still has plenty to do. Brown students have enough clout to influence city council elections. It's an easy commute to Boston, and weekend trips to NYC are cheap and easy. Less than an hour's drive gets you to at least three beaches in Rhode Island and Massachusetts."

Q "Personally, I can't imagine not going to school in a city. Brown is in the perfect location for a school. It is on a hill, so it seems secluded, but just **walking down the hill puts you in the center of downtown Providence**. Providence definitely has a city feel. There are always things to do and places to go. The Providence Place Mall, the largest mall in New England, is a 15-minute walk away."

Q "It's nice that there is a social life that revolves around the school. I started college at a big university in New York, and I always felt like people were off doing their own things in their own world. **Here, you really get to know the people in your class.**"

Q "There is the Trinity Repertory Company, which shows Broadway-caliber plays, the Fleet Skating Center, the Providence convention center, Waterplace Park, and many restaurants and parks. **Providence can be considered a college town** since, besides Brown, there is RISD, Providence College, and Johnston & Wales."

Q "The social options at Brown and in Providence are really very ideal. Many students become unhappy going to school in a small town where they are forced to stay on campus. Brown offers a wide array of on campus events, but **the city is so accessible if you are ever inclined to go off campus.**"

Q "**Providence is definitely a city that is on the up-and-up.** There are art galleries and neat movie theaters—both artsy, independent foreign places as well as multiple theaters that show Hollywood movies."

The College Prowler Take On...
Local Atmosphere

Providence is a city, but it's not a big city. Sometimes the desire for the city to grow and incorporate new and exciting features is at odds with its efforts to maintain the small-town feel. If you want to go to a club one night, a museum the next day, a hip-hop show and eat a few meals, you can cram it all into a weekend. Some Brown students never really explore the city, let alone the places less than an hour's drive in any direction from College Hill. There are beaches, state parks, ski areas, and vineyards close enough to make day trips to, all surrounded by quaint New England towns. Students complain about the lack of drive-in theaters or an all-night diner, without realizing that there are several of both about ten minutes away. There are more hip-hop, eighties, and live rock clubs and bars within walking distance of the University than Brown students can handle. And, of course, there is New York City and Boston, both easily accessible by bus and train for weekends when you need to get away.

Providence is a crowd pleaser. People from small towns may be a little intimidated at first, but except on goth night at Club Hell, the locals don't bite. Students from megalopolises such as New York, DC, or LA may scoff at the downtown area, which can be traversed in about 20 minutes, but no Brown student who puts in a little effort can honestly complain that there's nothing to do in Providence. The city simply has too much history, too many quirks, and too much to offer for the intrepid Brown student to find it boring.

A-

The College Prowler® Grade on

Local
Atmosphere: A-

A high Local Atmosphere grade indicates that the area surrounding campus is safe and scenic. Other factors include nearby attractions, proximity to other schools, and the town's attitude toward students.

Safety & Security

The Lowdown On...
Safety & Security

Number of Brown University Police:
22

Number of Additional Security Personnel:
18

Phone:
(401) 863-3103

Safety Services:
Blue-Light Phones
Emergency E-Mail Notification
Escort Service
Safe Walk Program
safeRIDE Shuttle

Health Services

24-hour EMS response

Allergy testing

Birth control counseling

Gynecological exams

Health forms for travel, employment, and school applications

Routine sports and travel physicals

STD screenings

Vaccines and medical prescriptions

Health Center Office Hours

Appointments for non-medical emergencies:

Monday and Friday 8:30 a.m–4.15 p.m.

Tuesday through Thursday 9:30 a.m.–4:15 p.m.

Students Speak Out On...
Safety & Security

> **"I feel safe here. Then again, I'm from New York City, so I feel safe just about anywhere."**

Q **"My computer got stolen freshman year from my room**. I left my window cracked open, and someone crawled in. My roommate had jewelry stolen at the same time. Still, I feel relatively safe on campus (I think security has improved since then). I walk home alone sometimes. I use the shuttles but not the Safe Walk program."

Q "I think that there are certain areas off campus that you should avoid when you are walking alone, but on campus, **you don't have to worry about much.**"

Q **"I never had a problem with security**. They respond well when you lock yourself out of your room and don't hassle you too much when drinking is involved. However, you have to watch your back at night because there have been a lot of muggings, and security isn't everywhere. There has also been much dispute over arming Brown police with firearms."

Q "There are security guys who hang around campus in yellow jackets at night. I think they are kind of useless. **The campus is very safe.** I like to go running and feel fine running all over the campus and the neighborhoods."

Q "On campus, things are pretty safe. In the nearby periphery, it is pretty **safe to walk alone at night.**"

Q "**Safety is not one of Brown's strong points**. It is, after all, located in the city. If you follow basic safety procedures, you should be fine. Walk in groups and stay in well-lit areas. Personally, I have never had any problems with it, and I don't know anybody who has. Providence is rated one of the safest cities in the United States, but it's still a city. You just have to keep your wits about you when you're walking around."

Q "I think it's good that **the University uses e-mail to keep us informed about crimes** going on around campus, but I think they are a little sensationalist, and they also make it sound worse than [the crime] actually was. In some of the situations I was actually part of the incident, but when I read the e-mails, I knew they made it sound worse than it actually was. It's no worse than most other urban schools."

Q "Last year it really felt like **there were e-mails coming every day about students getting jacked**."

Q "**I don't think there is a reason to feel unsafe**, but at the same time, if you are walking alone on Benefit Street at four in the morning on a Saturday and something happens to you, you cannot blame it on the area. You know the east is safer than any other area of Providence. I'm convinced that the men in yellow coats aren't doing much of anything."

The College Prowler Take On...
Safety & Security

Brown students receive an alert by e-mail every time there is a major crime committed on campus or the University perceives a specific safety threat. Recently, in response to a real and perceived increase in crime on and around campus, Brown increased the hours of campus police, hired security officers to patrol at night, and hired a private consulting firm to address the problems. The University tries very hard to inform the students about the status of crimes on campus and provides services to encourage smart and safe movement on campus at night. The shuttle runs on a route all the way around campus and comes about every five minutes until 3 a.m. The escort, who picks up and drops off students from off-campus housing to any location on campus, runs every night from 5 p.m. until 3 a.m. Safe Walk is a student-run volunteer program that provides walking escorts for students every night. Students should feel safe, but not be naïve about the threats that do exist in cities and on College Hill.

The campus area has all the common security features. There are many blue-light phones and well-lit public areas, and the police presence is generally strong enough to deter crime. Most students seem to feel very safe on campus and will admit that things like theft happen when doors are carelessly left unlocked or valuables are left in public places. Still, many students choose to leave their laptops unattended in the libraries or never lock their dorm rooms.

C+

The College Prowler® Grade on

Safety & Security: C+

A high grade in Safety & Security means that students generally feel safe, campus police are visible, blue-light phones and escort services are readily available, and safety precautions are not overly necessary.

Computers

The Lowdown On...
Computers

High-Speed Network?
Yes

Wireless Network?
Yes

Number of Labs:
9

Operating Systems:
Mac OS, UNIX, Windows

Number of Media Labs:
2

Number of Computers:
317

24-Hour Labs:
Center for Information Technology (CIT) Building

Charge to Print?

Yes. Single-sided pages are five cents, double-sided pages are seven cents. Each student is issued a $25 card at the begining of the year. These cards are called PAW Cards—People Against Waste.

Free Software

Programs include Adobe Acrobat Pro, Adobe Illustrator, Adobe Pagermaker, Adobe Photoshop, CS ChemDraw, ELFE, EndNote, Exceed, KaleidaGraph, Kedit, Dreamweaver, Mathematica, Matlab, PCTeX, ProDesktop, SAS, Scientific Word, SciFinder Scholar, Sigmaplot, SPSS, Symantec AntiVirus, and Tecplot.

For a full listing, visit *www.brown.edu/Facilities/CIS/Software_Services/software/supportlist.html.*

Did You Know?

Brown has a pioneering computer science department. One interesting ongoing project on campus is **the Cave**, an eight-foot cubicle where high-resolution stereo graphics are projected onto three walls and the floor to create a virtual-reality experience. The Cave is used for medical, archeological, artistic, and creative writing projects.

Students Speak Out On...
Computers

{ **"Most students have their own computers. There are enough clusters not to need one, but it just gets tight during exam periods and thesis due dates."**

Q "The computer network is **pretty good**, and I believe it will get better. Occasionally, the network shuts down, but they notify you ahead of time. It's best if you have a personal computer and printer because labs can get crowded at times."

Q "Bring your own computer. If you get a laptop, **buy a wireless card**, so you can get hooked up in the libraries."

Q "I brought my own computer but **I end up doing all my work at computer labs** because I can't get anything done in my dorm. I don't think it's essential to have a computer because the facilities are pretty extensive. During finals, it could be hard without one."

Q "The **networks are good**, and you get some space on the University's file server to save your files. I never used mine, but I knew I had it."

Q "I definitely think you need to bring your own computer to Brown. **The clusters are always full of people**. If I didn't have one, I think I would have turned a lot of papers in late. My roommate freshman year came to Brown without one, but she bought one within a month because she thought it was such a pain not to have one."

Q "Brown has computer clusters in the main libraries and the CIT (Center for Information Technology). **It is not absolutely necessary to have a computer on campus**. There are enough computers in the cluster to accommodate the ten percent of students who do not have their own computers."

Q "I'm a Mac user, and I've found that **there are fewer resources available to me**."

Q "I think **it's easy to use campus computers**. I haven't needed to have my own in my three years here."

Q "I think **having a computer makes it a lot easier**. I don't know anyone without a computer. I relied on the school's printers, but that's about it."

Q "Definitely bring your own computer. The computer clusters are accessible and generally easy to use, but in college, **everything depends on e-mail**—you need to be able to access it at any hour."

The College Prowler Take On...
Computers

Computers are a necessary tool at Brown. All papers, research, and communication revolve around having access to computers. The Center for Information Technology helps students adapt their own computers for use in the University network. Every Brown student has a University e-mail account, server space, and full access to most of the University's computer software and hardware. All of this is in addition to all the electronic research tools available through JOSIAH, the library Web site server. The CIT also holds free group and individual training sessions to help students use specific software that the University makes available through their network. Network security is high, which has the positive effect of keeping viruses and junk mail away from people's inboxes, but also has essentially cut off illegal file sharing on the University's network.

While many students get by without a computer, the majority of students either bring a computer or purchase one from either the Brown bookstore's computer center or a private company soon after they arrive. The fact that most students have their own computer decreases the traffic at the clusters at all but the busiest times of the year. If you are buying a new computer, a laptop is your best bet; it takes up less space in the cramped freshmen rooms and gives you the freedom to bring your computer to any of your favorite study spots. Brown's new wireless network also gives students the chance to access the Internet with their laptop in certain places on campus. In general, Brown's computers offer more resources than most students could ever desire, and the school continues to expand its computing facilities, taking advantage of new technology as it becomes available.

B+

The College Prowler® Grade on

Computers: B+

A high grade in Computers designates that computer labs are available, the computer network is easily accessible, and the campus' computing technology is up-to-date.

Facilities

The Lowdown On...
Facilities

Student Center:

Faunce House

Athletic Centers:

Bear's Lair Athletic Center

Meehan Auditorium Ice Rink

Olney-Margolies Athletic Center (OMAC)

Pembroke Field

Pizzitola Sports Center

Smith Swim Center

Libraries:

Anne Marie Brown Library

Art Slide Library at the List Art Center

John Carter Brown Library

The John D. Rockefeller Humanities Library (Rock)

John Hay Library (Special Collections)

Orwig Music Library

The Sciences Library (Sci-Li)

Campus Size:

140 acres

What Is There to Do?

There are more things happening on and around campus than you could ever hope to do. It is easy for students to start any kind of club or activity if it doesn't already exist on campus, which is unlikely considering there are over 200 official University-supported organizations. All these student interests are also provided proper meeting facilities. Once buildings close for the academic day, they remain open for organizations to use as meeting places. There are also several playhouses, music practice spaces, and studios for the artistically inclined.

Movie Theater on Campus?

The Brown Film Society has movie marathons in the evenings and on the weekend in Carmichael Auditorium.

Bowling on Campus?

No

Bar on Campus?

Brown currently enjoys two on-campus bars. The Graduate Center Bar, below the Graduate Center Dorm, was recently named one of the ten hippest college bars in the country. Known to students as the GCB, the bar donates thousands of dollars in profits to charity every year. The Hourglass Café and concert venue is a favorite of underclassmen. The café is entirely student staffed and managed, offering some of the best on-campus jobs.

Coffeehouse on Campus?

The Upper Blue Room in Faunce House is home to the University's main coffeehouse, but the Rockefeller Library also has a small coffee and snack shop in the lobby.

Students Speak Out On...
Facilities

> **"The athletic facilities need some improvement. Everything else is pretty good, in my opinion."**

Q "The facilities are very nice. They're very state-of-the-art and Ivy League-ish. **We don't have an official student center**, but Faunce Hall acts as one, since it houses the Student Activities Office, the mail room, a mini-arcade, the Campus Market, and various other things."

Q "I participate in gymnastics and **the facilities could use some attention**. We're donor funded, so our facilities compared to other school's gymnastics facilities are not the best. But we can deal with it, we're fine."

Q "The **campus is beautiful**. Enough said."

Q "**Nothing is crazy nice**. They are doing better jobs on newer classrooms, but most of the buildings from the '60s and '70s are pretty bad, but they are doing great things when they renovate halls. The athletic center is alright, the courts are good, but weight room and nautilus machines could use a new layout."

Q "**Brown needs a better central place**, something like a student center or rec center."

Q "The computer labs are nice, and there are a lot of them. I'm not an athlete, so I don't know much about the athletic facilities, but **the student center consists of a café, a market, and a bar**, which is open almost every night and is great if you can't muster the energy to go clubbing."

Q "Most things are fairly centralized, and the campus is fairly compact. The only thing is that **the athletic center can be a little bit of a walk** depending on where you are living. Nothing is more than ten minutes away, though."

Q "The **athletic facilities aren't the greatest or the newest**, but they get the job done. The computer labs are pretty good."

The College Prowler Take On...
Facilities

Brown's facilities reflect Brown student's needs; the average Brown student would tell you they spend much more time in the library than at the gym. Therefore, it makes sense that the libraries and computer centers are constantly renovated and updated, while other facilities may receive less attention. That being said, Brown is not completely lacking any facilities, but it is easy to see which interests are given priority.

Compared to other Ivies, Brown's facilities are modest and reflect a certain degree of frugality. A quick look at the campus will not necessarily showcase the hidden, but first-rate, costume shop, wood and metal working studio, or the special libraries. Most students have everything they need, though it may take them a little time to find it.

B

The College Prowler® Grade on

Facilities: B

A high Facilities grade indicates that the campus is aesthetically pleasing and well maintained, facilities are state-of-the-art, and libraries are exceptional. Other determining factors include the quality of both athletic and student centers and an abundance of things to do on campus.

Campus Dining

The Lowdown On...
Campus Dining

Freshman Meal Plan Requirement?
Yes

Meal Plan Average Cost:
$2,884

Places to Grab a Bite with Your Meal Plan:

The Blue Room
Food: Soups, sandwiches
Location: Faunce House, the Main Green
Favorite Dish: Focaccia chicken sandwich
Hours: Monday–Friday 7 a.m.–6 p.m.

Campus Market

Food: Cereal, dairy, dry goods

Location: Under the Blue Room

Favorite Dish: Energy bars

Hours: Monday–Friday 8 a.m.–11 p.m., Saturday–Sunday 2 p.m.–11 p.m.

The Gate

Food: Pizza, subs, ice cream

Location: Alumni Hall, Pembroke campus

Favorite Dish: Pizza, hot sandwiches

Hours: Monday–Friday 11 a.m.–2 a.m., Saturday 6 p.m.–2 a.m., Sunday 4 p.m.–2 a.m.

The Ivy Room

Food: Omelets, wraps, salad, pizza station, smoothie station

Location: Wriston Quad, below the Ratty

Favorite Dish: Smoothies, falafel

Hours: Monday–Friday Lunch: 11:30 a.m.–1:45 p.m., Snacks: 8 p.m.–12 a.m.

Josiah's (Jo's)

Food: Grill, sushi, wraps, soups

Location: Middle of Vartan Gregorion Quad

Favorite Dish: Beef Carberry with cheese

Hours: Daily 24 hours (food is not available 2 a.m.–6 a.m.)

The Sharpe Refectory (The Ratty)

Food: Grill, trattoria, vegetarian, and Kosher meals

Location: Wriston Quad, main campus

Favorite Dish: Chicken nuggets, magic bars

Hours: Monday–Saturday 7:30 a.m.–7:30 p.m., Sunday 10:30 a.m.–7:30 p.m.

The Verney-Woolley Dining Hall (The V-Dub)

Food: Fruit station, sandwich station, vegetarian meals

Location: Emery-Woolley Hall, Pembroke Campus

Favorite Dish: Cajun gumbo, tater tots

Hours: Monday–Friday 7:30 a.m.–9:30 a.m., 11 a.m.–2 p.m., 4:30 p.m.–7:30 p.m.

Off-Campus Places to Use Your Meal Plan

None

Student Favorites

The Blue Room, the Ivy Room, Josiah's

Other Options

If you can't leave campus to eat, you can take your chances with the notorious Haven Brothers silver truck, which parks in front of Wayland Arch on Wriston Quad most nights after 8 p.m. If you feel less adventurous, it is also easy to get Chinese and Italian food delivered to dorms. Finally, Café Carts at Barus & Holley, CIT, and the Rock are usually around offering coffee, sandwiches, and other snacks.

Did You Know?

There is a Ratty Recipe Repository link off of **Brown's Daily Jolt Web site** which has student-submitted recipes for meals using ingredients in the University's cafeteria. Recipes include "Curry Chicken Salad," "Fruity Desert Crepes," and "Macaratty and Cheese."

Students Speak Out On...
Campus Dining

> "The meal plan is all right. The V-Dub has recently been renovated, and their food is consistently tasty. Food quality at the Ratty, the other dining hall, is less consistent. But there is usually a decent selection."

Q "The main dining-hall food is **below average** to average cafeteria food. Special snack bars are pretty good and give you good variety."

Q "I hated meal plan when I was on it! **The Ratty is the pits, but I hear it got better**. The V-Dub is a better option. Josiah's and the Blue Room are better alternatives if you have points, and the Gate is a good place to get a piece of pizza."

Q "The **meal plan rips you off**. The Ratty was disgusting. I was on the full meal plan. I'm definitely going off of it even though I'm living in a dorm without a real kitchen, which should tell you something. I think the V-Dub is a little better. Being off meal plan without a car might be a little difficult."

Q "I stayed on meal plan for all three years that I lived in the dorms. It was great to get to see people in the dining halls. **There's usually something good to eat**."

Q "I think the **food got progressively worse** over the time I was on the plan. I'm excited to be off meal plan now."

Q "It would be **cheaper to go off the meal plan**, but there are tradeoffs. Now that I'm off meal plan, I eat whatever comes my way. If you don't have a car or access to a car, it would be really frustrating to be off the meal plan."

Q "I went to both cafeterias. I went to the Ratty more, but the V-Dub is nicer. **The atmosphere at the V-Dub is nice**; they play music, and it feels more like a restaurant. It's the same food no matter where you go."

Q "I was on full meal plan my freshman year. After that, I switched to seven meals. **I was done [with the meal plan] by junior year.**"

The College Prowler Take On...
Campus Dining

While most schools have contracted with Marriott or fast-food companies for their dining needs, Brown prides itself on maintaining a University-run food service. Why exactly this is a source of pride is another question entirely. The main dining halls—the Ratty and the V-Dub—serve what can only be described as average food. Chances are, you won't return home for the holidays demanding your mom cook more like Brown Food Services (BFS). A lack of variety and the inability to use credits in real restaurants close to campus can be frustrating. The few cafés and restaurants run by the University are equally frustrating because they are more expensive than independent cafés and diners on Thayer and Wickenden Street. The Brown meal plan feels more like a middle school lunch program than a welcomed dining experience.

Year after year, the Ratty is the butt of new and old jokes, but as demonstrated by the Ratty Recipe Repository, many Brown students embrace the standard cafeteria-style eating. Besides, the meal plan provides much more than hot food every day. The meal plan is a state of mind. From your first week on meal plan, you will undoubtedly enjoy meals with friends, meet lots of new people, and sing karaoke with your fellow Brunonians at the V-Dub. Good or bad, surviving meal plan freshman year is a defining experience and undoubtedly a right of passage. In time, however, you'll find the right balance of splurging for off-campus meals and eating creatively at the dining halls. Students who are off the meal plan might enjoy better food, but it is costly and time consuming to fend for yourself.

The College Prowler® Grade on
Campus Dining: C-

Our grade on Campus Dining addresses the quality of both school-owned dining halls and independent on-campus restaurants, as well as the price, availability, and variety of food.

Off-Campus Dining

The Lowdown On...
Off-Campus Dining

Restaurant Prowler:
Popular Places to Eat!

Al Forno

Food: Contemporary Italian

577 South Main St.
Downtown

(401) 273-9760

Cool Features: Nothing says your parents love you like a dinner excursion to Al Forno. Their brick-oven pizza is world-famous and the chocolate soufflé is a must.

(Al Forno, continued)

Price: $50 and under per person

Hours: Tuesday–Friday 5 p.m.–10 p.m., Saturday 4 p.m.–10 p.m.

Apsara

Food: Cambodian, Vietnamese, Thai, and Chinese

716 Public St.
Providence

(401) 785-1490

Cool Features: Although Apsara is a 10-minute drive from campus, it is so good that

→

(Apsara, continued)

Brown students cram into the restaurant every night.

Price: $10 and under per person

Hours: Sunday–Thursday 10:30 a.m.–9:30 p.m., Friday–Saturday 10:30 a.m.–10 p.m.

Bickford's Grille

Food: American

1460 Mineral Spring Ave. North Providence

(401) 353-9442

Cool Features: Known for great New England-style breakfast—which is to say breakfast with seafood integrated into it. Bickford's is also a great spot to hit after the bars on weekends; they also offer takeout, which is a big plus.

Price: $15 and under per person

Hours: Sunday–Thursday 7 a.m.– 7 p.m., Friday–Saturday 7 a.m.–3 a.m.

Café Paragon and Viva

Food: Mediterranean and American

234 Thayer St. College Hill

(401) 331-6200

Cool Features: Most famous Brown-frequented restaurant is and bar. The restaurant still proudly displays the 1999 *Vanity Fair* article that highlighted Paragon/Viva as

(Café Paragon, continued)

one of the favorite haunts for Brown's children of privilege. Despite this reputation, the food is very affordable. Paragon and Viva provide a great balance of affordable food with superb service, strong martinis, and an elusive indoor smoking section. After 10 p.m., Viva becomes a hip Euro club scene.

Price: $15 and under per person

Hours: Sunday–Thursday 11 a.m.–1 a.m., Friday–Saturday 11 a.m.–2 a.m.

Café Zog

Food: Café and coffee shop

239 Wickenden St. Providence

(401) 421-2213

Cool Features: Zog features a private back patio and table service.

Price: $7 and under per person

Hours: 7 a.m.–12 a.m. daily

The Creperie

Food: Crepes and smoothies

82 Fones Alley (off Thayer) College Hill

(401) 751-5536

Cool Features: Located right off Thayer Street, the Creperie is a great option for any meal of the day. Late hours make it one of the few places to get a post-bar snack.

Price: $7 and under per person

(The Creperie, continued)

Hours: Monday–Thursday 10 a.m.–12 a.m., Friday–Saturday 10 a.m.–2:30 a.m., Sunday 9 a.m.–12 a.m.

The Cuban Revolution

Food: Cuban

149 Washington St. Providence

(401) 331-8829

Cool Features: The brilliant cabana atmosphere with live music in the evenings makes eating a pressed Cuban sandwich, fried plantain chips, and flan a welcome treat. Wear camouflage on Saturdays or a Che Guevara print on Mondays for special discounts.

Price: $10 and under per person

Hours: Monday–Tuesday 11 a.m.–10 p.m., Wednesday–Saturday 11 a.m.–12 a.m.

East Side Pockets

Food: Middle Eastern

278 Thayer St. Providence

(401) 453-1100

Cool Features: East Side Pockets provides excellent service, great food, and personality that satisfies the demand for affordable munchies. The friendly family that runs East Side Pockets will have you in and out with a lamb, grape-leaf, or falafel pocket faster than you can say "pickles, peppers, humus, tabouli, tahini, hot sauce."

(East Side Pockets, continued)

Price: $5 and under per person

Hours: Monday–Thursday 10 a.m.–1 a.m., Friday–Saturday 10 a.m.–2 a.m., Sunday 10 a.m.–10 p.m.

Fellini Pizzeria

Food: Pizza

166 Wickenden St. Providence

(401) 751-6737

Cool Features: Fellini is ridiculously popular among students, and most agree it's some of the best pizza in New England (though it definitely has its detractors). It's particularly popular around midnight and thereafter on Fridays.

Price: $6 and under per person

Hours: Monday–Thursday 11 p.m.– 12 a.m., Friday 11 a.m.–2 a.m., Saturday–Sunday 12 p.m.–12 a.m.

The Garden Grille Café and Juice Bar

Food: Vegetarian and vegan cuisine

727 East Ave. Pawtucket

(401) 726-2826

Cool Features: Veggies and vegans can proudly take their carnivorous friends to this slightly out-of-the-way vegetarian restaurant.

(The Garden Grille Café and Juice Bar, continued)

The menu makes it easy for people with all kinds of dietary concerns to eat hearty and tasty meals like Vegan Nachos Supreme, a veggie Rueben or a slice of dark chocolate cake.

Price: $12 and under per person

Hours: Monday–Saturday 10 a.m.–9:30 p.m. (Juice bar opens at 11 a.m.)

Haven Brothers

Food: Diner

72 Spruce St. (sort of) Fulton and Dorrance Sts. Providence

(401) 861-7777

Cool Features: For starters, Haven Brothers is not as much a restaurant as a trolley with a diner in it. The establishment is over a hundred years old, and serves a very mixed crowd when it pulls up in front of City Hall and serves diner fare through the morning hours.

Price: $8 and under per person (cash only)

Hours: Usually along the lines of 5 p.m.–3 a.m.

Hemenway's Seafood Grill and Oyster Bar

Food: Seafood

121 South Main St. Providence

(401) 351-8570

(Hemenway's Seafood Grill and Oyster Bar, continued)

Cool Features: The raw bar at Hemenway's offers more than 15 varieties of raw shellfish, and the waterfront location makes it a great spot for hip students and Providence yuppies alike.

Price: $40 and under per person

Hours: Monday–Thursday 11:30 a.m.–10 p.m., Friday–Saturday 11:30 a.m.–11 p.m., Sunday 12 p.m.–9 p.m.

India

Food: Indian and Pakistani

123 Dorrance St. Downtown

(401) 278-2000

Cool Features: Providence, particularly the area around Brown, offers a few good Indian restaurants. Although India may be a few dollars more than other options, the food and the service make India the nicest choice.

Price: $25 and under per person

Hours: Monday–Thursday 11:30 a.m.–9 p.m., Friday–Saturday 11:30 a.m.–10 p.m.

Julian's

Food: Gourmet/fusion bistro food

318 Broadway Ave. Federal Hill

(401) 861-1770

(Julian's, continued)

Cool Features: Julian's is true boho Providence dining— greasy with a silver spoon. Breakfast is particularly good; you can get eggs benedict with lox and Bourson cheese hash served in a hip, artsy café.

Price: $15 and under per person

Hours: Monday–Thursday 9 a.m. to 11 p.m., Friday–Saturday 9 a.m.–2:45 p.m and 11 p.m.–1 a.m., Sunday 9 a.m.–2:45 p.m.

Mediterraneo

Food: Authentic Italian

134 Atwells Ave.
Federal Hill

(401) 331-7760

Cool Features: Federal Hill has an almost endless variety of Italian restaurants, but Mediterraneo is one off the few that features Italian speaking servers and authentic Tuscan cooking. Many of the eateries on Federal Hill claim to be worth their extravagant price, but Mediterraneo, with its enormous portions, truly is.

Price: $40 and under per person

Hours: Monday–Thursday 11:30 a.m.–9 p.m., Friday 11:30 a.m.–12 a.m., Saturday 12 p.m.–10 p.m., Sunday 4 p.m.–9 p.m.

Ri~Ra

Food: Irish Pub

50 Exchange Terrace
Downtown

(401) 272-1953

Cool Features: Ri~Ra is a lively pub which is a favorite of college students and the Providence happy-hour set. Once you live in Providence, you'll know how unusual that is.

Price: $15 and under per person

Hours: Sunday–Wednesday 11:30 a.m.–1 a.m.,Thursday–Saturday 11:30 a.m.–2 a.m.

Sawadee

Food: Thai

93 Hope St.
Providence

(401) 831-1122

Cool Features: While there are a few Thai restaurants around town, Brown students are lucky to have this authentic, family-run place so close to campus. The takeout is a godsend, and diners will be pleased to see the signature dishes served as spicy as they dare to request them.

Price: $12 and under per person

Hours: Call in advance, but dinner is almost always served from 5 p.m–9:30 p.m.

Spike's Junkyard Dogs

Food: All-American hot dogs

273 Thayer St.
College Hill

(401) 454-1459

Cool Features: Spike's has dozens of great theme hot dogs such as the Texas-Ranger (bacon bits, baked beans and BBQ sauce) and the Buffalo Dog (blue cheese,

(Spike's Junkyard Dogs)

wing sauce and scallions). Eat more dogs than anyone in the current hall of fame, and you will be immortalized in Spike's Kennel Club.

Price: $5 and under

Hours: Monday–Thursday 11 a.m.–12 a.m.,
Friday–Saturday 11 a.m.–3 a.m.

Closest Grocery Stores:

Eastside Marketplace
165 Pitman St.
(401) 831-7771

Super Stop & Shop
333 West River St.
(401) 861-9300

Whole Foods Market
261 Waterman St.
(401) 272-1690

Other Places to Check Out:

Antonio's, Au Bon Pain, Ben and Jerry's, Broad Street Tokyo, D'Angelo's, Johnny Rockets, Kabob and Curry, Meeting Street Café, Mia Sushi, Miss Fanny's Soul Food Kitchen, Sakura, Smoothie King, Ten Prime Steak & Sushi

Student Favorites:

East Side Pockets, India, Sawadee, Spike's Junkyard Dogs, Viva (at Café Paragon)

24-Hour Eating:

There's no 24-hour eating near Brown, but some late-night diners are Bickford's, Haven Brothers, and Fellini Pizzeria.

Best Pizza:

Al Forno

Best Chinese:

Apsara

Best Breakfast:

Julian's

Best Wings:

Ri~Ra

Best Healthy:

The Garden Grille Café

Best Place to Take Your Parents:

Hemenway's Seafood Grill and Oyster Bar

Mediterraneo

"On my Brown application, I literally said that one reason I wanted to come here was for the great Italian food in the area."

Q "The restaurants are very good; **that's one of the best parts about living in this city**. There are so many good places that I feel like I need a full four years to try them all. When you get to school, get an *Around and About Providence* book; it has all the listings of restaurants in the area. There are really too many good ones to name, but generally, I eat on Thayer Street, on Wickenden Street, or downtown. Federal Hill, Providence's Italian district, is a short trolley ride away and has fantastic Italian food. There are also some great Thai and Indian places, if you like those types of food."

Q "The restaurants are great. Thayer and Wickenden streets are good and close. Paragon is great and cheap. Also check out Sakura for sushi and Federal Hill for more expensive Italian food. **Providence also has great Indian and Thai food**. Just steer clear of Chinese."

Q **"I've always been amazed at the variety of restaurants** Providence has to offer. My favorites are the Italian restaurants and the Paragon burger. There is great variety, and Providence is small enough to try and digest most of it."

Q "My favorite restaurant that I can never go to because it's so expensive is Ten Prime Steak & Sushi. **I go when my dad comes into town**."

Q "Thayer Street is the 'college town' street of Brown. **There are lots of restaurants, small sandwich shops, and chains**. Paragon's a nice sit-down place that's not too expensive. D'Angelo's, Au Bon Pain, Smoothie King, Ben and Jerry's, Johnny Rockets, East Side Pockets, Antonio's Pizza, and Kabob and Curry are the chains. Meeting Street Café has really great, mega-sized sandwiches and cookies; if it's your birthday, they give you a free cookie."

Q "It has a lot of **good breakfast places**."

Q "Providence can be **kind of expensive**, and the food can be a little monotonous."

Q "Off-campus food is spectacular. **There is a ridiculous amount of really good restaurants** in the area since Johnston & Wales serves up so many good local chefs. Fast-food places are all over the place; there's falafel, pizza, and pastries everywhere. You won't have to worry about having variety."

Q "Sawadee has **amazing Masaman curry**."

Q "**Miss Fanny's Soul Food Kitchen is amazing**. Broad Street Tokyo is good for sushi, as is Mia Sushi on Federal Hill."

The College Prowler Take On...
Off-Campus Dining

Providence truly caters to the epicurean diner. One need not stray further than the College Hill and the Downtown areas to find all varieties of ethnic food, dining styles and atmospheres. Without a doubt, Providence is host to an impressive number of off-campus restaurants that offer variety in terms of price and menus. Vegetarian, Kosher, and all other diets can be easily accommodated. Great food is truly one of Providence's greatest assets.

The scariest thing about off-campus eating, however, is the lack of supermarkets that are easily within walking distance. The closest supermarket is over a mile away, which will sound a lot worse in February when it snows and gets dark before dinner. There are a few specialty markets nearby, including a Saturday farmers market at Hope High School, but you really need a car if you plan to cook on a regular basis.

The College Prowler® Grade on

Off-Campus Dining: A-

A high Off-Campus Dining grade implies that off-campus restaurants are affordable, accessible, and worth visiting. Other factors include the variety of cuisine and the availability of alternative options (vegetarian, vegan, Kosher, etc.).

Campus Housing

The Lowdown On...
Campus Housing

Undergrads on Campus:
80%

Best Dorms:
Barbour Hall
Young Orchard Apartments

Worst Dorms:
New Pembroke
Perkins Hall

Number of Dormitories/Houses:
27

Number of University-Owned Apartments:
40

Dormitories:

Andrews Hall

Floors: 3

Total Occupancy: 166

Bathrooms: Shared by floor

Coed: Yes

Residents: Freshmen, sophomores, juniors, seniors

Room Types: Upperclassman singles and freshman doubles

Special Features: Each room has a sink with a medicine chest, which is very rare for freshmen rooms.

Barbour Hall Apartments

Floors: 2

Total Occupancy: 129

Bathrooms: Private

Coed: Yes

Residents: Sophomores

Room Types: Apartments

Special Features: Each apartment has a kitchen, common room, and a private bathrooms.

Barbour Hall Dormitory

Floors: 1

Total Occupancy: 37

Bathrooms: Shared with adjoined room

Coed: Yes, by room

Residents: Sophomores

Room Types: Singles and doubles

(Barbour Hall Dormitory, continued)

Special Features: Every room shares a sink, toilet, and shower with one other room. Rooms also feature an enormous walk-in closet.

Caswell Hall

Floors: 4

Total Occupancy: 90

Bathrooms: Shared by floor

Coed: Yes, by room

Residents: Sophomores

Room Types: Doubles

Special Features: Caswell is split into three towers, and each room has a non-working, but atmospheric, fireplace.

Emery-Woolley Hall

Floors: 4

Total Occupancy: 227

Bathrooms: Shared by a cluster of about six students

Coed: Yes, by room

Residents: Freshmen, sophomores, juniors, seniors

Room Types: Singles and doubles

Special Features: In the coldest depths of winter, living in the same building as the V-Dub Cafeteria will make you the envy of Pembroke Campus. There is also a huge common room with a working fireplace and an elevator.

Graduate Center Suites

Floors: 4 to 5

Total Occupancy: 120

Bathrooms: Shared by suite

Coed: By suite

Residents: Mostly sophomores, some juniors and seniors

Room Types: Suites with singles

Special Features: It might look a little like a prison, but it provides a good way for sophomores to get singles.

Hegemen

Floors: 4

Total Occupancy: 70

Bathrooms: Shared by suite

Coed: Yes

Residents: Sophomores, juniors, seniors

Room Types: Suites with mostly singles, some independent singles and doubles

Special Features: The five Hegemen towers are connected by tunnels that are underground.

Hope College

Floors: 4

Total Occupancy: 76

Bathrooms: Shared by floor

Coed: Yes, by room

Residents: Freshmen, sophomores, juniors, seniors

Room Types: Singles and doubles

(Hope College, continued)

Special Features: Hope College is conveniently located on the Main Green, and residents can look forward to a year of leisurely strolling from their bedroom to classes.

Keeney Quad (Archibald, Bronson, Everett, Jameson, Mead, and Poland)

Floors: 4

Total Occupancy: 597

Bathrooms: Shared by floor

Coed: Yes

Residents: Freshmen, sophomores, juniors, seniors

Room Types: Singles, doubles and triples

Special Features: About half of the freshmen class lives in the Keeney megaplex. To support so many, the dorm has a lot of common rooms, storage rooms, kitchens and has two private quads.

Littlefield Hall

Floors: 4

Total Occupancy: 50

Bathrooms: Shared by floor

Coed: Yes

Residents: Freshmen

Room Types: Doubles

Special Features: Littlefield is open for winter break to house student athletes; if you're not a jock, you might have one staying in your room over the holidays.

Metcalf Hall

Floors: 4

Total Occupancy: 60

Bathrooms: Vary by floor

Coed: By floor

Residents: Sophomores, juniors, seniors

Room Types: Singles

Special Features: Metcalf is a quiet dorm ideal for serious students or light sleepers. The top floor of singles is reserved exclusively for female students.

Miller Hall

Floors: 4

Total Occupancy: 55

Bathrooms: Shared by floor

Coed: Yes

Residents: Graduate students

Room Types: Singles

Special Features: Miller includes laundry facilities and services, kitchens, an Ethernet connection in each room.

Minden Hall

Floors: 6

Total Occupancy: 80

Bathrooms: Shared by suite

Coed: By suite

Residents: Sophomores, juniors, seniors

Room Types: Suites and singles

Special Features: Minden is a newer addition and was renovated in 2002.

(Minden Hall, continued)

Residents believe it is among the best housing at Brown. The top floors have great views of the city, but not all suites have equal accommodations. When choosing Minden in the lottery, scope out the rooms first.

Morris-Champlin

Floors: 4

Total Occupancy: 200

Bathrooms: Shared by cluster

Coed: Yes

Residents: Freshmen, sophomores, juniors, seniors

Room Types: Singles, doubles and suites

Special Features: This is one of the few dorms to have an elevator, which makes moving in a breeze. Since the first floor of Champlin used to be the Pembroke infirmary, some rooms on the first floor have their own bathroom.

New Pembroke 1, 2, 3, 4

Floors: 4

Total Occupancy: 193

Bathrooms: Shared by floor

Coed: Yes, by room

Residents: Freshmen, sophomores, juniors, seniors

Room Types: Singles and doubles

Special Features: New Pembroke may be at the edge of Pembroke campus, but it is literally on Thayer Street and close to restaurants and stores.

Perkins Hall

Floors: 4

Total Occupancy: 275

Bathrooms: Shared by floor

Coed: Yes, by room

Residents: Freshmen

Room Types: Singles
and doubles

Special Features: Perkins
is strictly first-year housing
shared only with upper-class
counselors. It is one of the
furthest dorms from campus,
but it is known for its
breeding camaraderie.

Slater Hall

Floors: 4

Total Occupancy: 50

Bathrooms: Shared by floor

Coed: Yes, by suite

Residents: Juniors, seniors

Room Types: Singles, doubles,
and triples

Special Features: This is a
favorite of juniors and seniors
because it is located right on
the Main Green. Rooms are also
spacious with high ceilings and
great views.

Vartan Gregorian Quad

Floors: 4

Total Occupancy: 290

Bathrooms: Shared by floor

Coed: Yes, by room

Residents: Sophomores, juniors,
and seniors

Room Types: Three-, four-, five-,
and six-person suites

(Vartan Gregorian Quad, continued)

Special Features: This housing
complex forms a quad, and
Josiah's is conveniently located
in the center. Residents enjoy
the use of elevators and large
common rooms in their suites.
The quad also houses the
Brown Hotel where your parents
can stay at a bargain price.

Wriston Quad (Buxton, Chapin, Diman, Goddard, Harkness, Marcy, Olney, Sears, Wayland)

Floors: 4 to 5

Total Occupancy: 743

Bathrooms: Shared by floor
or suite

Coed: Yes, by room

Residents: Freshmen,
sophomores, juniors, seniors

Room Types: Singles, doubles,
and suites of varying sizes

Special Features: Wriston Quad
has the advantage of being
near campus and the main
dining hall. The singles and
doubles are nothing special, but
the suites on the top floors are
arguably the nicest at Brown.
All of the buildings except for
Wayland, Buxton, and Harkness
house Brown's meager Greek
system. Fraternities or sororities
usually occupy the lower floors
of the buildings, but they do
not dominate the scene except
during weekend parties.

Young Orchard Apartments

Floors: 4

Total Occupancy: 190

Bathrooms: Shared by apartment

Coed: Yes

Residents: Sophomores, juniors, seniors

Room Types: Apartments

Special features: Basically the same as living in an off-campus apartment, but it is close enough to campus that students don't have to worry about transportation.

Students Living in:

Singles: 39%

Doubles: 47%

Triples/Suites: 4%

Apartments: 10%

Bed Type

Twin extra-long.

Available for Rent

You can rent microwaves and small refrigerators from the Brown Student Agency. The same goes for towels and sheets.

Cleaning Service?

Most dorms have a custodial service that keeps hallways, bathrooms, and other public areas reasonably clean.

What You Get

Every room has a phone jack, an Ethernet hub, and free cable with access to Brown's HBO-like movie channel. Rooms also come with a lamp or an overhead light, a desk, a dresser, a book shelf, and a bed.

Also Available

Although every dorm has laundry machines, laundry service is also available through the Brown Student Agency.

Room Types

Standard – Students share a large central bathroom facility. Most first-year students are assigned to these rooms.

Suites – Several students share a suite, which has single or double bedrooms, a common room, and a sink area without a toilet.

Apartments – Several students share an apartment, which has all singles, a kitchen, a common room, and a full bathroom.

Houses – A large group of students share a full, University-owned house. Each house has its own unique features, but students enjoy the advantages of living in a house without the hassles of moving off campus.

Program Houses

Program Houses are a major alternative to the housing system and encorporates Greek organizations and Theme Houses. Many students choose to join these houses after their freshman year because the housing lottery favors juniors and seniors, leaving sophomores with the worst choices. Program Houses are a way to circumvent the lottery and wind up in a place you actually like.

111 Brown Street and Plantations House – In addition to program houses and co-op living, Brown offers a couple of on-campus houses to groups of about 15 sophomores who collectively enter a lottery for the houses. Competition for these houses varies by year, but usually rising sophomores either do not know about the option or cannot get enough friends together to enter the lottery. Students who are lucky enough to win the lottery get to live in a Victorian mansion with 15 of their closest friends. Historically, these houses throw great parties almost every week.

BACH (Brown Association for Cooperative Housing) – Brown has two official co-op houses which are non-profit organizations. Co-op residents are responsible for all their own cooking, cleaning, and general maintenance. They are Watermyn (166 Waterman Street) and Finlandia (116 Waterman Street).

Bottega-Olney House (Wriston Quad) – Bottega is a program house dedicated to promoting creative expression within the house, the Brown community, and the surrounding community.

Buxton International House (Wriston Quad) – The objective of Buxton house is to bring together enthusiastic, internationally-minded people under one roof to promote cultural exchange through events such as dinners, study breaks, community service, and parties. About half the residents are from the United States and half are international students.

Greek Houses – Greek houses at Brown, for the most part, help create a diverse community in which they can participate in community service, scholarship, social activities, and friendships. In addition to fraternities and sororities, Brown has coed societies in its Greek system. All fraternities and sororities are located in dormitories around Wriston Quad and share the buildings with non-Greek students.

Harambee House (Wriston Quad) – Harambee, which means "togetherness" in Swahili, brings together people interested in the politics, culture, society and other aspects of African culture, and attempts to inspire a sense of community, academic excellence, and leadership for all people of African decent. House members participate in the organization and implementation of community service and educational, social, and cultural events.

Harkness Technology House (Wriston Quad) – The tech house provides a place for Brown students interested in science and technology to share tools, skills, ideas, and enthusiasm. Members particularly enjoy sharing the house's high-tech gadgets. You don't even need to be an engineer or computer science major to live there.

Machado House (87 Prospect Street) – Machado House is a huge mansion about four blocks from the Main Green where Brown students interested in the language and culture of the French-speaking and Spanish-speaking worlds live together. House events open to all of the Brown community include "pain et fromage" nights, cuisine nights, fiestas, and ciné-club screenings. You should speak French or Spanish to live here, so it is a great place to build your language skills.

Marcy Games House (Wriston Quad) – The philosophy of Marcy House is that games are one of the most enjoyable forms of social interaction and are an art form that can be a powerful cornerstone for community living. Residents engage in board games, card games, role-playing games, computer games, and many others to inspire a friendly and fun social atmosphere.

St. Anthony Hall at King House (154 Hope Street) – St. Anthony is a national, co-ed literary fraternity that uses literature and learning to build a community of friends both inside and outside the house.

West House/Environmental House (91 Brown Street) – West House is a small community of about a dozen Brown students who strive to create a tight-knit group of students interested in simple living, vegetarian co-op cooking, and environmentalism.

Did You Know?

Campus housing is the source of many of Brown's most popular rumors. There is **a highly mysterious tunnel system** that connects a good deal of Wriston Quad to the Greek and Program houses. There are endless theories about the original intent of these tunnels, but rumor has it they used to extend over a large portion of the school.

Brown is also said to have a few secret societies in addition to the well-publicized organizations; these societies are said to be located near campus in mysterious mansions. The most famous myth concerns the ominous Graduate Center Suites. It is rumored to have been designed in 1968 by prison architects as a fortress in case of riots. Regardless of the building's design intent, it is a fact that the imposing concrete spiral staircase was actually built incorrectly because the builders read the blueprints wrong.

After talking so much about housing, Brown students have **come up with their own terms** for Brown's sometimes odd dorms. A "dingle" is a room originally built as a double which has been converted to a single. A "trouble" is a room originally built as a double which has been converted to a triple.

Adding to the eccentricity of the Brown housing system, Residential Life sponsors a **lip-synching contest** each year in February. The prize, which can go to any group, including rising sophomores, is selecting any on-campus room, suite, or apartment. As you would expect, this is a competitive contest.

Students Speak Out On...
Campus Housing

> **"Dorms are pretty decent. Some are much nicer than others, though. As a freshman, you'd want to be in Keeney—that's where most freshmen are, and it's located on the convenient side of campus."**

Q "All **freshmen dorms are fine**. Don't worry if you get a so-called 'bad dorm' because you end up bonding with your dormmates over that anyway. There is a housing shortage, but it's really the sophomores that get screwed. As a freshman, you have no control over what dorm you get, so don't worry about it."

Q "Emery Woolley and Mo-Champ used to be super-gross, a **bad '70s public-housing project**. They refurnished them well. I'll cheer Keeney for its social, thirsty, and frisky freshmen. Since you don't pick housing as a freshman, have faith in Residential Life. Andrews has really nice rooms, but it's pretty quiet."

Q "I am staying on campus senior year. I live in Slater Hall, right next to University Hall, and I definitely don't want to move. I can roll out of bed and into my classes. **My room is large, with high ceilings**, and I get a view of sunset down College Hill."

Q "The dorms at Brown are very **huge and very pretty**."

Q "The dorms aren't bad, and **many freshman rooms are actually very nice**. As a freshman, everyone is assigned a roommate and a dorm, so you have no say in the matter. No matter what, housing is guaranteed all four years."

Q "**I've stayed on campus all four years**. I don't want to have to pay bills. I have the rest of my life to deal with real life. For a year, I feel like it's not worth it to buy a bed and furniture—and the senior dorms are nicer than a house off campus anyway. I don't see the point when the houses are right next door to the dorms anyway."

Q "**The dorms are good** and the unit, our freshman hall, creates some of your closest friends ever."

Q "As a frosh, Keeney and Andrews are great for social scene, **Perkins kind of sucks**, but other people who lived there liked it."

Q "**I loved living in the dorms**. I lived in Perkins freshman year. I always traveled in a group with my friends that were in my freshmen unit. A lot of the people I lived with first year grouped together and got a suite on campus sophomore year. We took up a whole floor of a dorm. I got to know a lot of people and made friends in my freshman unit."

The College Prowler Take On...
Campus Housing

Brown guarantees housing for four years if the student wants it. They also require students to live on campus for the first six semesters of their Brown career. Although many students complain about this policy, it makes life easier for rising sophomores and juniors, and relieves a lot of the stress between freshman and junior year. Starting in the spring of freshman year, students are faced with a lot of choices in terms of housing. In addition to the lottery, all the program and Greek houses give students the choice of getting around the fickle lottery system. In addition to circumventing the lottery, special housing is one more chance to meet new people and have new experiences.

Despite complaints about the frustrating lottery system, Brown's housing system is better than most. After freshman year, the system can be worked to a student's advantage—including some houses reserved specifically for sophomores. Live in the dorms first year. Live in a house sophomore year. Move to a different program house junior year if you didn't love your sophomore digs. By senior year, you'll skip the whole lottery system and will be guaranteed prime on-campus housing without ever being forced to enter the lottery or move off campus. A little finesse is all it takes to make the housing system work for you.

B+

The College Prowler® Grade on

Campus Housing: B+

A high Campus Housing grade indicates that dorms are clean, well-maintained, and spacious. Other determining factors include variety of dorms, proximity to classes, and social atmosphere.

Off-Campus Housing

The Lowdown On...
Off-Campus Housing

Undergrads in Off-Campus Housing:
20%

Average Rent For:
Studio Apt.: $600/month
1BR Apt.: $800/month
2BR Apt.: $1200/month

Popular Areas:
Brook and Cushing Streets, right off Thayer

Fox Point, around Governor Street

Wickenden Street Area

Best Time to Look for a Place:
For the best selection, look no later than February; however, if you want the best prices, wait until late in the spring when the landlords are anxious to rent their spaces.

For Assistance Contact

Residential Life

www.brown.edu/Administration/ResLife/grapevine/offcampus.html

(401) 863-3500

Res_Life@brown.edu

Students Speak Out On...
Off-Campus Housing

"Off campus is only available for seniors, but it is definitely the way to go if you can. Just make sure your landlord and neighbors aren't too insane because that does happen."

Q "It's definitely worth it. **Most people live within a 5- or 10-minute walk from campus**. Then there are loft and other house/apartment options in the city if you want to pay less, have more space, and have more of a blank canvas to work with."

Q "**I lived off campus one year, and it was awesome**. I lived in Young Orchard the year before—that was a step down, but only a very small step."

Q "I lived off campus for two years. **Off-campus living is totally better**. The annoying thing was, I had to stay in dorms until my junior year. I would have moved off earlier if I could have."

Q "Many juniors and seniors live in off-campus housing. There seems to be **enough to go around**, and it's pretty nice, pretty affordable, and very convenient and close to campus. The campus is very compact, so nothing is a very far walk."

Q "Living off campus, I get more studio space and cheaper digs. **No one's in my business**."

Q "Off-campus housing can be **extremely convenient**; it's as close to campus as a dorm. Of course, the farther away from campus you go, the cheaper it is. But, most students that live off campus find the walking commute minimal."

Q "**I've never felt at home on campus**. But, living off campus, I'm not as likely to go to things on campus late at night."

Q "**More freedom**. You are treated like an adult, not a student."

The College Prowler Take On...
Off-Campus Housing

Brown guarantees housing for all four years, even though most students opt to live on their own by senior year to gain more freedom, more space, or better facilities. Some years, the University lets juniors live off campus too, but officially, only seniors are guaranteed permission. Students apply to the Office of Residential Life for off-campus permission in the early spring of their junior year, most having already signed a lease in the previous months. As a senior, getting permission is easy, but finding the perfect apartment can be a greater challenge. Within a mile radius of campus there are endless housing options, but the best places are rarely advertised. Hit the pavement or ask friends if you want to find the best place. In general, students can find any kind of place they want—historic houses, new apartments, studios, or mansions.

While most students believe they save money by moving off campus, the frustrations and complications of moving off campus often add up quickly. Summer subletting can be hard, and don't forget the astronomical heating bills during the long winter. Moving off campus should be a careful choice. Since the University requires students to live on campus for a few years, it's easy to know if moving away from the University bubble is right for you.

The College Prowler® Grade on

Off-Campus Housing: A-

A high grade in Off-Campus Housing indicates that apartments are of high quality, close to campus, affordable, and easy to secure.

Diversity

The Lowdown On...
Diversity

Asian American:
14%

White:
65%

African American:
7%

International:
6%

Native American:
1%

Out-of-State:
94%

Hispanic:
7%

Political Activity

Brown is famed for its political activism and liberal atmosphere, but actual activism and demonstrations on campus have become more infrequent. While it is common to find students discussing politics and volunteering for liberal causes, rallies and sit-ins are part of Brown's past.

Gay Pride

Brown students and faculty are extremely receptive and friendly to all people, and there have been very few incidences of discrimination or hate crimes related to sexual orientation. The effort to promote queer politics and acceptance is spearheaded by the Queer Alliance. Twice a year, the organization hosts a huge dance that is among the most popular campus parties.

Most Popular Religions

Brown does not have a single predominant religion, and the majority of students claim to have no particular affiliation. However, sources show that some religious minorities have particularly high numbers at Brown. Services are provided for students of all religions; they list Bahat, Buddhism, Christianity, Hinduism, Islam, Jainism, Judaism, and Sikhism as the most popular Brown faiths.

Economic Status

Brown recently made a major admissions policy change to accept students on a "need-blind" bases in order to promote quality of scholarship and demonstrated ability above affluence. However, the average Brown student comes from the upper-middle class.

Minority Clubs

The Third World Center at Brown was created in 1976 to meet the needs of all minority students and promote racial and ethnic pluralism in the Brown community. Minority students receive a great deal of support from the Third World Transition Program: the presence of Minority Peer Councelors in freshmen dorms, student publications such as the *African Sun* and *Somos*, and program houses such as Harambee House.

Students Speak Out On...
Diversity

{ **"The campus is somewhat diverse. There are a lot of people of Asian decent, but other races and ethnicities are underrepresented."**

Q "Diverse compared to what? Compared to Berkeley, it's not diverse. **Compared to Princeton, it's very diverse**. I don't know; people have different opinions on this, too."

Q "Brown has a **diversity of opinions and political views**, as well as students with all types of geographical, religious, racial, and educational backgrounds. If you want to meet people different form you, you have to make an effort."

Q "Brown is **not as diverse as it claims to be**, especially not economically."

Q "The University is an interesting size. It's small enough that you recognize a lot of faces on campus, but your social circle doesn't change that much. You always have a home base, but **I engage with a lot of people**."

Q "It's not terrible. We're doing okay by the percentages. But it's very hard to be here and forget that you are in very white, very middle-class New England. I don't think it's an us-versus-them environment, but the manifestation of relations, either racial or class, exist."

Q "There is not enough **political diversity among the professors**, and certainly not among the students."

Q "There are two indications that **race is still an issue around campus**. One, there is still a lot of dialogue between the students and the administration on the subject; but also, the overwhelming sense of mistrust that most white students show when it comes to minorities. I think a lot of students feel that there might be overcompensation and that white problems, whatever those are, are not addressed."

Q "Brown is diverse. I would say **we are the most genuinely diverse student body**. We also have every possible student activity that you could want. If we don't have it, it's easy to start your own and get funding."

Q "Frankly, in terms of Brown's image, once you get here you realize that **there are so many pockets**, like hippies and hipsters. It's all here."

The College Prowler Take On...
Diversity

Brown makes an honest effort to promote socioeconomic diversity in the student body; the recent change to need-blind admissions is just one example of this goal. Also, a recent endowment (the biggest single gift ever made to Brown) promises to preserve the goal of providing financial aid to deserving students. While the hard numbers indicate that there is a good deal of racial and economic diversity at Brown, the day-to-day interactions between students are the real test of diversity and tolerance at Brown. There a very few outright problems or public sentiments that indicate a lack of diversity at Brown. In spite of this, students do not necessarily integrate themselves in their social circles.

The University gives Brown the basic ingredients to enjoy diversity in political, economic, racial, and geographical areas. It also provides support for students who come from a variety of backgrounds. Regardless of background, every student will be in a situation where they are confronted with people and opinions that they have never experienced before coming here. The vocal nature of Brown students and the University's outstanding policies, which protect freedom of student expression, mean that the school is as diverse as the students here make it.

B

The College Prowler® Grade on

Diversity: B

A high grade in Diversity indicates that ethnic minorities and international students have a notable presence on campus and that students of different economic backgrounds, religious beliefs, and sexual preferences are well-represented.

Guys & Girls

The Lowdown On...
Guys & Girls

Men Undergrads:
46%

Women Undergrads:
54%

Birth Control Available?
Yes

Social Scene

Brown students generally can be put into two groups: social butterflies and social caterpillars. It makes for a great dynamic. Just when you think you've exhausted your social sphere, you meet someone in a class who, it turns out, lived down the hall from you for two years but never left their room. That being said, freshmen housing units are the basis for future social interaction at Brown. In freshmen units, personalities spill into the hallways and start friendships that may last a lifetime. At Brown, a smile really is all it takes to meet people.

Hookups or Relationships?

Brown is a school where hookups reign supreme. Most students would say that they are simply too busy and too involved to pursue a committed relationship. Brown also seems to attract many freshmen with little or no relationship experience. It's impossible to say what combination of factors lead to the two most common sentiments about Brown students and dating: "there is no dating at Brown," and "we're just friends with benefits."

Did You Know?

Top Three Places to Find Hotties:

1. Thayer Street, Max's, and Viva
2. Wriston Quad
3. The Main Green

Top Five Places to Hook Up:

1. The 12th floor of the Sci-Li
2. The Underground
3. The GCB
4. A freshmen lounge
5. The Main Green

Best Place to Meet Guys/Girls

Students spend most of their time on campus, so the back row of a lecture hall, a small study section, or an all-night study group are all great places to start relationships. The same goes for the libraries and cafés on Thayer Street. The fact that few students leave campus on the weekends means that the students looking for a good time will be concentrated at one of the half-dozen big and easy to find parties on any given night.

Dress Code

Unshaved armpits and dreadlocks will always be a staple of the Brown hippie look, but Brown guys and girls exhibit the full range of styles and attitudes. Fake Prada and Louis Vuitton mix with real high-fashion looks. There's everything from boarding-school kids who can't shake their preppy duds to the dirty hippy garb that really makes you question whether all dorms are equipped with showers. Unfortunately, the cold weather can get the better of fashion during the winter months, but the dress code for those who care is either designer head-to-toe or funky and artsy. In May, shorts and short skirts distinguish between those that spring-breaked in the Bahamas and those that stayed on campus to work on their thesis. The fashionable Brown guy looks a bit euro, a bit bohemian, or classic Abercrombie. For girls, there's everything from perfectly coifed designer looks to oblivious fashion victims. The fashionable Brown girl, above all, strives for her own unique style. Collectively, Brown kids definitely rock a style.

Students Speak Out On...
Guys & Girls

> "The social life is fun, though there isn't a ton of dating at Brown. There are plenty of attractive people here. Like everything at Brown, you have to be persistent. The social life revolves around the school."

Q "I'd have to say the **guys at Brown are hotter** than the girls. It's not exactly a big dating school, but people do date and hook up."

Q "I haven't had too much success with girls at Brown. Freshman year I had a girlfriend. That was about it. **I meet most girls at parties**."

Q "I don't know how much of a dating scene there is, but there's certainly **enough action to go around**."

Q "Once you find a good one, **you should hold on to her**."

Q "Beautiful women. **So many beautiful women**."

Q "I always had a good time at parties, as long as I stayed away from Greek life. It's **unclear how much actual dating is taking place**."

Q "I don't know much about dating at Brown. The girls are cool. **I can't complain**. Try dating around RISD."

Q "There are some cool girls, and there are interesting people. **Good diversity**."

Q "**Guys at Brown are flaky**. I've dated enough to know. I've met a lot of people that are socially awkward, but I think that's why we get along so well. It's funny when they all come together."

Q "The **guys at Brown are a lot cooler than the girls** at Brown."

Q "There are two kinds of relationships here: major serial monogamy and **screwing a lot of people**."

Q "No serious dating. Not here. I think there's a variety of guys. Some guys like to take girls out on dates. A lot of guys don't; **they're more into the hook-up thing**. I think that there is more going here than at most places. It happens pretty often; it's definitely common."

Q "We're certainly hotter than Harvard or Columbia. Dating depends on your clique. **There's a lot of sex**, but I don't know how many relationships there are."

Q "I know a lot of people who have been **dating the same person for three years**."

Q "Brown is one of those places where **you meet really cool people**, but there's not so much casual dating going on. You are either in a long-term relationship or single."

Q "There are **some cute guys**."

The College Prowler Take On...
Guys & Girls

According to the rumors, the headshots Brown requires with every application are meant to ensure Brown's reputation for having the most attractive Ivy League students. Whether or not you believe this rumor is entirely a matter of taste (and whether you consider "attractive Ivy League student" an oxymoron). In general, students tend to agree that the admissions office did a fabulous job choosing interesting and enjoyable classmates, but they are a little more critical when it comes to sharing anything more than intellectual curiosity with their peers. However, the truth of the matter is that the Brown student body is no more or less attractive than any other population of 20-year-old students; observers are just as likely to rave about the spectacular beauties lounging on the Main Green as they are to complain about the pale, four-eyed creatures that wander out of the library late at night.

The only real consensus is on the state of the dating scene: there isn't one. Students chose between serial relationships, random hookups, or celibacy. While this is a common complaint on Friday nights, the system is probably perpetuated because it suits the busy Brown lifestyle.

The College Prowler® Grade on

Guys: B+

A high grade for Guys indicates that the male population on campus is attractive, smart, friendly, and engaging; and that the school has a decent ratio of guys to girls.

The College Prowler® Grade on

Girls: B

A high grade for Girls not only implies that the women on campus are attractive, smart, friendly, and engaging; but also that there is a fair ratio of girls to guys.

Athletics

The Lowdown On...
Athletics

Athletic Division:
NCAA Division I

Conference:
Ivy League

School Mascot:
The Brown Bear

Males Playing Varsity Sports:
400 (15%)

Females Playing Varsity Sports:
437 (14%)

→

Men's Varsity Sports:

Baseball
Basketball
Crew
Cross-Country
Diving
Equestrian
Fencing
Football
Golf
Ice Hockey
Lacrosse
Skiing
Soccer
Squash
Swimming
Tennis
Track and Field
Water Polo
Wrestling

Women's Varsity Sports:

Basketball
Cross-Country
Diving
Fencing
Field Hockey
Golf
Gymnastics
Ice Hockey

(Women's Varsity Sports, continued)

Lacrosse
Skiing
Soccer
Softball
Squash
Swimming
Tennis
Track and Field
Water Polo

Club Sports:

Basketball
Rugby (Men's)
Sailing
Soccer
Tennis
Ultimate Frisbee (Men's)
Ultimate Frisbee (Women's)
Volleyball (Men's)

Intramurals:

Basketball
Football
Frisbee
Hockey
Soccer
Softball
Squash
Tennis
Volleyball

Athletic Fields

Pembroke Field, Stevenson Field, Warner Roof Field

Getting Tickets

Since most varsity athletic events are only moderately attended, it is only hard to get tickets for the biggest games of the year. In most cases, showing up to an event with your Brown ID is all you need to get in. For information, call (401) 863-2773.

Most Popular Sports

Despite the fact that many Brown teams are highly ranked in any given season, there is a relatively low amount of student support for varsity athletic events. Big games against other Ivy League teams, however, draw big crowds. IM and club Frisbee, basketball, and football foster a lot of positive competition.

Best Place to Take a Walk

A walk through campus and the surrounding neighborhoods features a variety of historic buildings. For a more athletic run, try the trails around India Point Park or Blackstone Boulevard.

Gyms/Facilities

Hunter S. Marston Boathouse

The men's and women's crew teams house their boats in this waterside facility about two miles from campus. The boathouse, in addition to housing the team's vessels, has a workshop, a 16-seat rowing tank, and 34 rowing machines.

Olney-Margolies Athletic Center (The OMAC)

The OMAC is the main gym on campus. It features a 200-meter indoor track, five indoor tennis courts, and many varsity training facilities, as well as IM and club competition grounds.

Pizzitola Sports Center

The Pizzitola Sports Center provides an intercollegiate competition court for men's and women's basketball, volleyball, wrestling, and gymnastics, and has bleachers for 2,800 fans. This center also contains the Washington Weight Room.

Smith Swim Center

Boasting a long and short course pool, as well as a complete diving well and sauna, the Smith Swim Center is an under-used asset in the Brown athletic complex. In addition to the pool facilities, there are also eight squash/handball courts.

Students Speak Out On...
Athletics

> "Varsity sports are definitely present, and they're a good program if that's your thing. Intramurals are so much fun, and a lot of kids get into basketball, football, softball, and Frisbee."

Q "Intramurals are pretty popular. **Varsity sports are almost like a social scene**, and like all other social scenes, it's fractious and segregated from most other things. Part of the reason is that there's less of a stigma for athletes; it's more that the sports complex is not physically in the center of campus."

Q "Club sports are a lot of fun without the pressure of varsity sports. There's a **huge culture that revolves around the ultimate Frisbee teams**. I play club ultimate Frisbee. There's no varsity team, but the club team travels a lot."

Q "**What's a varsity sport**? No, seriously, if you're looking for colleges where you can be a celebrity on campus because you are an athlete, then look elsewhere. My friends that are varsity athletes work very hard, and it is difficult for them to have social lives outside of their teams. Some of them end up dropping the team; others have a great experience so they stick with it and love their teammates and their sport."

Q "At the beginning of each semester, **professors let athletes know that if there's a conflict to let them know about it**. They're willing to work with us and it's definitely supportive. It's not like there's a vendetta there or anything."

Q "It's hard playing on a varsity team sometimes because we travel a lot. My social life is somewhat hindered because during the season, I can't go out on a Friday night like most people. On the other hand, I'm hanging out with a bunch of people I wouldn't know otherwise. It affects me academically. It makes me focus my time a lot. **I know if I wasn't playing a sport I wouldn't learn to manage my time as well**. I would procrastinate a lot."

Q "I'm too weak to play real football. Coming to Brown and finding intramural football was **a shining star in my athletic career**."

Q "I played low intensity IM basketball. It was **tons of fun**."

Q "Some teams take **a lot of walk-ons**."

Q "If I wasn't playing a sport, I would have time to take photography. But in general, I think I can do just about **everything I want to do at the University and still be a varsity athlete**. I'm still a double concentrator."

Q "A lot of students just don't know about Brown athletics at all. **Only the biggest games are well attended**."

Q "The only thing I don't like about Brown is the way the athletes are treated here. **I'm an athlete, and people only assume I got in because I'm an athlete and I'm in dumb-jock classes**. There's a lot of hostility to athletes here; not from the professors but sometimes from other students. I feel like the athletes do as well in classes, if not better than non-athletes."

Q "It can be **as intense as you want it to be**. There's a really great community of people who are athletically-minded but want something less intense than varsity but still highly competitive."

The College Prowler Take On...
Athletics

Brown is not an overly athletic school. Almost every student played some varsity sport in high school, but for most students, academics and other extra-curricular activities come before athletics. However, there are a full range of varsity sports and less intense club and intramural sports. Many Brown students go for runs around campus, or they find themselves playing catch or Frisbee on the Main Green.

Sports are just one aspect of social life. They help relieve stress from the academic rigors of the University. Brown has facilities for non-athletes to swim, workout, and play organized sports. Brown also has gifted student athletes who may go underappreciated despite winning records.

The College Prowler® Grade on
Athletics: C+

A high grade in Athletics indicates that students have school spirit, sports programs are respected, games are well-attended, and intramurals are a prominent part of student life.

Nightlife

The Lowdown On...
Nightlife

Club and Bar Prowler:
Popular Nightlife Spots!

Club Crawler:

Brown students definitely spend more time in bars than clubs. The hip-hop scene around campus is stronger at on-campus parties spun by student DJs. The occasional RISD warehouse party is an event not to be missed, if you catch wind of it and are able to find it.

(Club Crawler, continued)

Most students party within walking distance of the campus, but there aren't too many big dance clubs that merit the trip off campus. Keep in mind, all clubs and bars close at 1 a.m. from Sunday through Thursday, and at 2 a.m. on Friday and Saturday.

→

Club Hell

73 Richmond St.
Providence

(401) 351-1977

www.club-hell.com

Club Hell hosts the retro
and fetish club scene in
Providence. Although it's
no closer than any other
downtown night spot, Hell
attracts a good number
of Brown students, and
maintains a good balance of
edgy and accessible.

Cover ranges from $4 to $6

Tuesday: Underground
eighties, Hell's busiest
night. Bust a move or bang
heads to the Ramones, the
Cramps, Bowie, and their
contemporaries.

Sunday: Resurrection,
Providence's goth night.

The Complex

180 Pine St.
Downtown

(401) 751-4263

www.thecomplexri.com

A Providence dance staple,
the Complex promises to suit
almost any taste in its boring,
yet crowd pleasing, ways.
ladies night and college
night keep the students
coming, and the meager
five-dollar cover gets them
in and dancing.

(The Complex, continued)

Casual dress, casual looks,
and casual interaction.It's
unlikely that you'll run into
many other Brown kids, but
sometimes that's a good
thing. If you are looking to
cut loose Thursday–Saturday,
the Complex is a safe bet.

Thursday–Saturday $5 cover.

Fish Company

515 South Water St.
Providence

(401) 421-5796

Despite the admittedly
disgusting name, the Fish
Company is not a packing
house by day turned club at
night (although that might
give it a bit more mystique).
This is a club that Brown kids
frequent, most likely because
it's close to campus and easy
to find. Drinks might not be
cheap enough, considering
the very casual atmosphere,
but at least you can get fresh
air on the deck, which has a
nice view of the river.

Wednesday: Live Music.

Thursday–Saturday: DJ.

Lupo's at the Strand

70 Washington St.
Providence

(401) 245-9840

www.lupos.com

The granddaddy of Providence nightlife, Lupo's is a world-famous concert venue, bar, and occasional dance floor. A great place to catch soon-to-be-huge bands, Lupo's consistently pleases with a perfect lineup of hot bands, has-beens, and second-rate groups ranging from hip-hop and reggae to indie rock and ska. The Met Café, Lupo's sibling club, promises smaller, intimate shows with a full bar right next door.

Metropolis

127 Friendship St.
Providence

(401) 454-5483

Metropolis promises to be a hard-hitting club. Metropolis lives up to its name with multiple dance floors and spinning DJs. Grab your trendiest gear and a crisp Hamilton; ten bucks gets you in this big-city dance club. It tries hard to mimic the New York club feel, but it's only open Thursday–Saturday.

Pulse

86 Crary St.
Downtown

(401) 272-2133

Go-go boys and sweat-drenched bodies are the fare at Pulse, one of Rhode Island's largest gay clubs. Features all-male reviews.

Thursday: Karaoke with denise. No cover before 10.

Friday: Hetero-a-Go-Go. All persuasions welcome.

Viva

234 Thayer St.
Middle of campus

(401) 331-6200

Viva has been on campus for ten years, and based on the line to get in on Saturday nights, it's not leaving any time soon. There's no denying that Viva found its clientele in Brown's club-hungry international students. From the looks of it, you'll think you walked into a wormhole and were instantly transported to a glamorous city. Strong drinks, thick smoke, and even thicker accents are the scene. It's a see-and-be-seen hotspot. And don't even think about wearing those sneakers.

Open seven nights a week with a variable cover.

Bar Prowler:

While Viva may be the only club full of Brown students, other bars are frequented by Brown students any night of the week all over town. You can do a lot of damage with $20 at some popular Brown bars, or easily spend $100 on one bottle of wine in one of a dozen swanky bars and restaurants, most located around Federal Hill. Here are a few of the best.

Grad Center Bar

90 Thayer St.
On campus

(401) 421-0270

Nothing says get sauced like cheap drinks, cheap pool, and a bar that opens at four in the afternoon. The GCB is a great place for students to share a pitcher with their professors, TAs, or classmates. Unfortunately for most underclassmen, they are serious about IDs. Memberships to the GCB can be purchased with $20, a Brown ID, and driver's license.

Kartabar

284 Thayer St.
Providence

(401) 331-8111

www.kartabar.com

Popular for its boutique-chic atmosphere and its signature drinks, Kartabar is another stop along the Thayer Street bar scene. Students have strong drinks and see bafflingly overdressed patrons sip martinis and snack on European appetizers.

Liquid Lounge

165 Angell St.
On campus

(401) 621-8752

Smack in the middle of campus, Liquid Lounge's neon lights call to Brown students looking for a chill bar experience. Here the local and college crowd mix like oil and water, but everyone can get hosed together on dollar Rolling Rocks while listening to a rocking juke box.

Nick-a-Nees

76 South St.
Providence

(401) 861-7290

Although it's a little out of the way, Brown students occasionally pack its long tables, which are inevitably laden with peanut shells and the occasional broken glass. It's not much to look at, but Brown students dig dive bars, and Nick-a-Nees has dived about as far as it can go. Sometimes friendly staff, cheap eats, and live blues and rock bands make the bar a welcomed change from the packed college bars only a few miles away.

Patrick's Pub

381 Smith St.
Cranston

(401) 751-1553

Patrick's has become something of a Providence staple, if not to Brown students in particular. Saturday night is college night, cover is $2 instead of $5 if you wear green.

The Red Fez

49 Peck St.
Providence

(401) 272-1212

Another wonderful dive bar, the Red Fez features a short bar and church-pew-style seating that makes you wonder if you've found the last-bastion for nerd glasses and MC5 T-shirts. Regardless, a semi-cold can of Schlitz for a buck and a half is enough to lure Brown hipsters downtown for a drink where nobody knows your name.

Steam Alley

520 S. Water St.
Providence

(401) 751-1820

Steam Alley is just a few blocks farther than most Brown students wander, but is less than a block from the ever-popular Fish Company. This relaxing bar has multiple big-screen TVs, cheap pool tables, and karaoke.

Tortilla Flats

355 Hope St.
Providence

(401) 751-6777

www.tortillaflatsri.com

Only a few blocks form Brown's campus, Tortilla Flats may seem like a godsend for anyone who notices the

(Tortilla Flats, continued)

conspicuous lack of Mexican food around campus. Sadly, nada mucho here, as far as food goes. The extensive line-up of tequila bottles, however, will leave you spinning like a piñata on Cinco de Mayo.

Trinity Brewhouse

186 Fountain St.
Providence

www.trinitybrewhouse.com

(401) 453-2337

A downtown microbrew, Trinity Brewhouse features patio seating in the heart of downtown. On Tuesdays, you can get a scenic tour of the facility, but the bar is a great place to grab a pint any day of the week.

Wickenden Pub

320 Wickenden St.
Providence

(401) 861-2555

The Wick Pub is close to a lot of off-campus housing. The drinks aren't cheap, but if you want to feel like you're drinking in the hull of a ship, they've got you covered. The pub showcases over 100 different bottles of beer in their front window, and you can join the Pint Club by drinking all of them.

The Wild Colonial Tavern

250 S. Water St.
Providence

(401) 621-5644

Voted one of the 50 best bars in America, the Wild Colonial is run by Brown professors. Pints of Guinness and darts abound at the foot of College Hill.

Student Favorites:

Fish Company

Grad Center Bar

Max's

Nick-a-Nees

Trinity Brewhouse

Viva

Useful Resources for Nightlife:

Brown's Daily Jolt

www.brown.dailyjolt.com

Bars Close At:

1 a.m. on weeknights,
2 a.m. on weekends

Primary Areas with Nightlife:

Thayer Street

Point Street Bridge area

Downtown

Wickenden Street

Cheapest Place to Get a Drink:

Grad Center Bar

The Red Fez

Favorite Drinking Games:

Beirut Beer Pong

Card Games (A$$hole, Kings)

Power Hour

Quarters

Upside-Down Alex

What to Do if You're Not 21

Club Hell and Fish Company both have good 18-and-up events on a weekly basis. In addition, check out:

Trinity Repertory

201 Washington St.
Providence

(401) 351-4242

Trinity Reparatory Company performs first-class theater performances produced by its own resident acting company. They features classics as well as contemporary works by local, national, and international playwrites, and it has special offers.

Underground AS220

121 Empire St.
Downtown

(401) 861-9190

Although it's a bar, AS220 is always all-ages and drinking really is only part of the scene.

Frats

See the Greek section!

Students Speak Out On...
Nightlife

"Parties on campus range widely and are widely dispersed. The frats are definitely not the main places to go for parties, unless that's your scene."

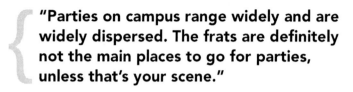

Q "I've never been to a club. Actually, I went to Viva once and never went back. **I'm a big fan of the GCB**."

Q "**Providence is a fun city**. There are lots of bars within walking distance of campus. It cuts down on driving. There are places to drink around town for freshmen."

Q "**Bars on campus are really easy to get into**. The main ones are Kartabar, Liquid Lounge, and Viva. Kartabar and Viva have Euro and Latin music on weekends, and Max's has hip-hop night and '80s night during the week. Downtown, there are a bunch of places that you can get into if your ID is remotely okay."

Q "If you like dive bars, Providence is a great place to be. **There are good cheap bars**."

Q "I go out Thursday nights. **I go to places that are close and don't have a cover charge**. There are a lot of places that are 18 and over. There are places to go to, but in general, I would spend most of my weekends in the dorms with my friends."

Q "There are certain places I like to go around campus because I have no ID problems there. **My roommate was Greek, so we spent a lot of time at Viva**."

Q "There's a **variety of different late-night scenes** at Brown—bars, clubs, pubs, snack bars, frat parties, and campus events—whatever suits you."

Q "The **on-campus parties are worth checking out** for underclassmen, but they're ultimately uninspiring and repetitive. House parties are great, as are a few bars and clubs. Check out Nick-a-Nees, the Red Fez, the Underground, when it's open, and the GCB."

Q "There are **some great bars around town**. I love Patrick's. I used to go to there by myself on Saturday mornings to watch soccer. It would be 10 a.m. on a Saturday, and it would be me, the bartender, and an 80-year-old man. I would ask for breakfast, and the bartender would offer me a beer with it."

The College Prowler Take On...
Nightlife

Brown students are fonder of bars than clubs. However, if you really need to party every night, Providence has a few dozen clubs that will expose you to Rhode Island nightlife, which can be gritty but holds promise for hot people and decent tunes. If drinking is all you need, Providence's bars, like its restaurants, cater to all styles and tastes.

Although Brown students are not the most adventurous, the bars, clubs, and other nightlife activities lurking in the city can entertain the blandest or wildest tastes any night of the week. Everyday, bars are swinging on College Hill, downtown and everywhere else in the city until at least one in the morning. Brown students who think that there's not enough to do after the sun goes down need to open their eyes, expand their bubble, and venture out to one of Providence's eager-to-please nightspots.

B+

The College Prowler® Grade on
Nightlife: B+

A high grade in Nightlife indicates that there are many bars and clubs in the area that are easily accessible and affordable. Other determining factors include the number of options for the under-21 crowd and the prevalence of house parties.

Greek Life

The Lowdown On...
Greek Life

**Number of
Fraternities:**
6

**Number of
Sororities:**
2

**Number of Coed
Greek Organizations:**
2

**Undergrad Men
in Fraternities:**
5%

**Undergrad Women
in Sororities:**
1%

→

Fraternities on Campus:

Alpha Epsilon Pi

Delta Phi

Delta Tau

Phi Kappa Psi

Sigma Chi

Theta Delta Chi

Sororities on Campus:

Alpha Chi Omega

Kappa Alpha Theta

Coeds:

Alpha Delta Phi

Zeta Delta Xi

Other Greek Organizations:

Alpha Theta

Greek Council

Greek Peer Advisors

Interfraternity Council

Order of Omega

Panhellenic Council

Pi Beta Phi

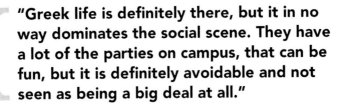

Students Speak Out On...
Greek Life

"Greek life is definitely there, but it in no way dominates the social scene. They have a lot of the parties on campus, that can be fun, but it is definitely avoidable and not seen as being a big deal at all."

Q "I **don't know anything about Greek life** at Brown."

Q "The Greek life is there for parties and some other events, but **it doesn't dominate**. It's not a big deal if you are in a frat or sorority, and it is not a big deal if you never set foot in one. No one cares one way or another. It's nice because you can go to frat parties, which can be fun sometimes, but it's not a status thing at all. However, there definitely are a few real 'frat' types, but it's nice to have a little bit of every type at Brown."

Q "Greek life is an option, but it doesn't dominate the social scene and it is avoidable. **Frat parties get old quickly**."

Q "I'm in a fraternity. I never thought I would join one, but it turns out that I did. They definitely do not dominate, but **they do provide big parties open to the whole campus** that a lot of people find to be pretty fun—there's dancing, drinking, and usually some theme. There's usually always something else going on around campus, though, and bars are always open."

Q "I feel like only about six percent of people live in fraternities and sororities, so **it's a small part of the scene**. You really have to search pretty hard to find someone who is involved in them."

Q "It exists, but it's not big. I think it's mostly a thing for freshmen. It's not like other schools where it's probably cool to be in a sorority. I never considered joining a sorority. **Freshman year, I went to a lot of fraternity parties, but I haven't been to one since**. All the other students and organizations throw just as many good parties, so I haven't been to one since freshman year."

Q "I wasn't in a sorority, but I lived in a dorm that was partially joined with a Greek house. Going into it I was very skeptical because you hear so many stories based on stereotypes, and living in a dorm with them changed my perspective of Greek life. They were very approachable. **It was intimidating at first**, I thought they were going to be rowdy, but in the end it created a great dynamic."

Q "There are always frat parties to go to if you don't have an ID. **They are pretty fun, all the same**."

Q "I lived in Bodega House, the creative expression house, which is not Greek life. It was a program house sandwiched between a normal frat and non-affiliated residents. **Brown put a revolving door between our space and the frat's**, and right away we felt physically separated. To counter the sense of separation, we had residential programmers who planned activities for the people in the building."

The College Prowler Take On...
Greek Life

Greek life at Brown is about as minimized as it can be. This is due to the Greek system itself and the University's attempts to seamlessly integrate frats and sororities into daily campus life. All Greek houses are on campus and abide by the same rules and regulations as any other organization on campus. The parties, for the most part, are open and welcoming to all students. If students never want to see the Greek system, they can easily ignore it. On the flip side, if students want a real Greek experience, they can find it in one of the dozen houses that do exist.

The Greek system at Brown is one of the many positive interest-groups. Banners hang around the Main Green and Wriston Quad to inform students of coming parties and events. A handful of nights during the year, you see the crazy, *Animal House*-type antics that Greek systems present at any school. However, if you want a school where you are defined by the three Greek letters printed on your T-shirt, Brown is simply not the place.

The College Prowler® Grade on

Greek Life: C+

A high grade in Greek Life indicates that sororities and fraternities are not only present, but also active on campus. Other determining factors include the variety of houses available and the respect the Greek community receives from the rest of the campus.

Drug Scene

The Lowdown On...
Drug Scene

Most Prevalent Drugs on Campus:

Alcohol

Cocaine

Marijuana

Speed

Study Drugs

Liquor-Related Referrals:

204

Liquor-Related Arrests:

0

Drug-Related Referrals:

108

Drug-Related Arrests:

2

Drug Counseling Programs

Brown's health service provides information about substance abuse as well as other common health issues for college students through its health education office, located on the third floor of health services. In addition, every freshman dorm has many undergraduate councelors who help students and provide a source of information on substance abuse issues. The phone number is (401) 863-2794.

Students Speak Out On...
Drug Scene

"If you want to find the scene, you can find it pretty quickly. If you don't want to, you can stay away from it. People are pretty open about their personal habits."

Q "I think **the policy is lax, and I like it**. I got in trouble once, but nothing came of it."

Q "Pot is the most used and accessible illicit drug at Brown. However, **coke, acid, mushrooms, and ecstasy also seem to be around** from time to time. The scene is avoidable if you so choose. I haven't really heard anything about heroin, which is a good thing."

Q "Yeah, most of my friends smoke and drink. **I wouldn't date someone who doesn't smoke or drink**, I think it's like that at most universities. I have friends outside of that group that I meet in class or at work to get a cup of coffee with, but people kind of stick to their circles here."

Q "**I've been brought in by Brown police** and security four times for smoking grass. Now I live off campus."

Q "I've **never been busted**. You hear stuff like that happening. I think Brown is really cool. They definitely give you a lot of responsibility, and they're pretty hands off. They expect students to make the right decision."

Q "Most Brown students are **responsible** about drinking and drugs."

Q "I would say **most students do drink**, but not a lot. I would say the average student would, at most, have four drinks—I mean in a night, not in an hour."

Q "**A fair number of people smoke pot**. It's not as many as those who drink, but I think a fair number of people do."

Q "Pretty easy to do, **pretty easy to get away with**."

The College Prowler Take On...
Drug Scene

While you can guarantee some exposure to drugs, it is by no means a social prerequisite. There is enough to do at Brown and in Providence to stave off the boredom that makes the drug scene thrive at other less-entertaining schools. Brown students, like any college student body, look to drugs for both social and academic reasons. Many students drink and smoke cigarettes and pot casually. From there, the scenes are more obscure and are neither prominent nor hard to find. Students at Brown tend to view substance use and abuse as a luxury that can be enjoyed with personal responsibility. The effects that abuse will have on your work and the threat of University and police action if you get caught keep students using drugs sensibly on campus.

In the end, students are neither excluded nor included socially based purely on their drug habits, and Brown students exhibit the full spectrum of personal habits. The most important thing to remember is that most Brown students are responsible and goal-driven kids. Drug use is more a by-product of college life than a main activity.

B

The College Prowler® Grade on

Drug Scene: B

A high grade in the Drug Scene indicates that drugs are not a noticeable part of campus life; drug use is not visible, and no pressure to use them seems to exist.

Campus
Strictness

The Lowdown On...
Campus Strictness

What Are You Most Likely to Get Caught Doing on Campus?

- Smoking cigarettes in the dorms.
- Smoking pot in the dorms.

Students Speak Out On...
Campus Strictness

> "You get in trouble if caught, but usually a first offense is only a hearing and a slap on the wrist. If you are careful and don't do that sort of stuff in public, the police won't bother you."

Q "My best friend at school had a few parties that were broken up, but somebody called the police because of the noise. **Brown is a very liberal school**; students are trusted to make their own decisions."

Q "Police are not strict at all. Whereas most schools have RAs or proctors in the dormitories who play the disciplinary role regarding drugs and alcohol, Brown has residential councelors, but they are mostly sophomores, and they do not play a disciplinary role at all. They are there only as peer advisors for when you need to talk or need help adjusting to school. **No one is there to tell you what to do**."

Q "Sometimes I felt like **they were out to get me**. We got busted once or twice, and then it seemed like the cops made a habit of coming by my room. We had some close calls, but we still got away with a lot."

Q "They're not strict about drinking. **With smoking, they've buckled down a little, but not much**. You will never go to jail, but maybe just get a dean's hearing."

Q "**Police generally don't look for people** doing stuff. But it's not like they'll pretend they didn't see it if they happen to come upon it."

Q "Campus was **too strict for me**. I couldn't wait to get away where no one patrols your lifestyle everyday."

Q "If they don't see it, they can't do anything. I was a residential counselor last year, and I had the same policy: **don't show me and I won't do anything**."

Q "They're **very loose about drinking** and things like that. There are no RAs either."

Q "Many times, if you are caught drinking, the cops tell you to just pour it out and leave. **It's pretty laid back**. Brown also doesn't have RAs in the normal sense. We have an MPC (minority peer counselor), a WPC (women's peer counselor), and an RC (resident counselor). Each exists in a freshman unit, and they don't write people up or report you. Their job is to advise you to make good decisions."

Q "Drug and drinking rules are **not heavily enforced here** in the slightest."

Q "**Don't worry about it**. They make sure you are safe and okay, and that is about it. We are a very loose school."

The College Prowler Take On...
Campus Strictness

The Brown police are not unlike those cool parents you knew in high school: they let the kids have their parties and almost never check out suspicious smells. While the police will nab students for any blatant displays of illegal behavior, they are unlikely to look for it unless staff or students notify them. These days, the main job of the Brown police is crime prevention and not student supervision. In addition, the counselor support system in the dorms provides a safe, open, and fun environment for the students, not a tool for the University to keep an eye on the students in their rooms.

Although many people do think enforcement is lax, people do go to dean's hearings and letters of reprimand are issued every time. The first few offenses stay confidential, but if the school is aware of a real problem, they will notify your parents and require counseling for social and substance-related issues. Blatant acts of crime against other students, on the other hand, are dealt with more harshly. The University establishes safe, yet liberal, boundaries for students and uses security presence to protect, not police, the students.

The College Prowler® Grade on

Campus Strictness: B+

A high Campus Strictness grade implies an overall lenient atmosphere; police and RAs are fairly tolerant, and the administration's rules are flexible.

Parking

The Lowdown On...
Parking

Student Parking Lot?
Yes

Freshmen Allowed to Park?
No

Approximate Parking Permit Cost:
$200–$385

Parking & Transportation Services:
Brown University Police and Security
75 Charleslfield St.
(401) 863-3157

Parking Permits

Permits and spaces are handed out through a seniority basis lottery. The lottery is held the second Monday of April for spaces to be given out the following year. Freshmen who bring cars to campus are not given access to the official Brown parking system. Frankly, having a car is not feasible or convenient until junior year.

Best Places to Find a Parking Spot

There are a few good secret spots in alleys or on un-metered streets, and if you are patient, you can circle the campus a few times and usually find something. The meters are poorly placed and usually broken, so the odds of getting a completely free space are good, but you will have to move your car every two hours. As you get farther from campus, the time limits become more liberal, the spaces more plentiful, and the odds of getting ticketed much lower.

Good Luck Getting a Parking Spot Here

On a rainy or snowy day, don't even think about trying to drive in and find a spot around campus or on Thayer. On most days, however, the two-hour parking limit keeps cars shuffling and makes the dismal prospect of finding a spot evenly difficult anywhere around campus.

Common Parking Tickets

Expired Meter: $10

No Parking Zone: $15

Handicapped Zone: $50

Brown Lots Without a Permit: $25 (1st offense), $50 (2nd offense), $75 (each additional)

Students Speak Out On...
Parking

"Don't bring a car. Parking is not the greatest, but you don't need a car because everything is walkable."

Q "Parking is **difficult but possible**! After freshman year, you can enter the parking lottery and get a reserved spot for the following year."

Q "It is **not easy to park if you are a freshman**. In fact, you are not allowed to have a car the first semester, so the people who do end up moving their cars to different places early in the morning. However, it really is not necessary to have a car. Basically everything is within walking distance, and Providence has a very good trolley system that takes you around for 50 cents. The campus is also a 15-minute walk from the train station, which has very cheap commuter trains to Boston. And the bus station is about a 10-minute walk away. Transportation is really convenient."

Q "Parking is tight in Providence. It is best to **get a spot through Brown** because you will get a $10 ticket if you park at night on the street."

Q "You sign up to receive a parking spot ahead of time, and then you get assigned to a lot, so **there's always a spot for you** there. But it's kind of tough to park anywhere else during the day."

Q "I have a car, but I hate driving. I walk everywhere. **Usually I use University lots**. It hasn't been broken into, but I've had lots of hubcaps stolen."

Q "Sometimes they raffle off parking spots at the end of the year, but if you don't have a spot, **plan on getting ticketed all the time**."

Q "Having a car is a beautiful thing, but **be prepared to fight tickets in court**. I think I pay, in tickets, what it would cost to buy a space. Most people park on the streets and pay the price."

Q "Fortunately, **I have always been able to get on-campus parking** or parking through local landlords who rent out a space for a semester. But if that doesn't work out, the Brown shuttle is great for taking you anywhere around campus. It runs pretty frequently—maybe every 10 minutes or so. There are also trolleys that can take you downtown to the mall, bars, clubs, and restaurants."

Q "Parking can be a pain, but you can pay for a parking spot through the school. But yeah, overall, **parking is annoying**."

The College Prowler Take On...
Parking

Do you like your car? Do you have a financial or emotional incentive to keep it in peak condition? Have you become accustomed to convenient and free parking? If you answered "yes" to any of these questions, you might want to seriously reconsider bringing your car to campus. The cruel winters and even crueler parking cops make street parking a dangerous proposition. If a snowplow doesn't hit your car, a $10 ticket will. It's widely known that the Providence city government is funded largely on parking tickets. Having a car, therefore, will probably cost you another 50 dollars a month in parking tickets. It's not as bad as the big cities, but you will start to get frustrated with the little orange friends you find on your windshield.

Brown parking also leaves a lot to be desired. Upperclassmen are usually able to get a university parking spot in a safe, covered lot, but there are far fewer good spots than students who want them. Most underclassmen are forced to park in a lot that's so far away it is only accessible by car. Private parking lots are the most popular choice for students, but they come at a high cost; some are $100 a month. Most students choose not to bring a car until senior year when they can park at an off-campus house or get a good university parking spot.

The College Prowler® Grade on

Parking: C+

A high grade in the Parking section indicates that parking is both available and affordable, and that parking enforcement isn't overly severe.

Transportation

The Lowdown On...
Transportation

Ways to Get Around Town:

On Campus
Brown Shuttle Service
Daily 5 p.m.–3 a.m.
The shuttle runs a set route around campus with 12 stops and promises no more than a seven-minute wait. Riders must show IDs to board.

BrownMed/Downcity Express
Transportation for Brown/ RISD medical students to local hospitals.

Brown Escort Service
Daily 5 p.m.–3 a.m.
This service provides transportation between University buildings and off-campus residences that are within the service's boundaries.
(401) 863-1778

Public Transportation
Rhode Island Public Transit Authority (RIPTA)
(401) 781-9400
Check out the full listings for local and regional buses at *www.brown.dailyjolt.com/ transportation*

Taxi Cabs

AAA Ace Taxi:
(401) 331-6667

Checker Cab Co.:
(401) 273-2222

Economy Cab:
(401) 944-6700

Metro Taxi:
(401) 331-8888

East Side Taxi:
(401) 521-4200

Yellow Cab Inc.:
(401) 941-1122

Car Rentals

Alamo Rent-A-Car
local: (401) 435-7447
national: (800) 327-9633
www.alamo.com

Avis
local: (401) 521-6197
national: (800) 831-2847
www.avis.com

Enterprise
local: (401) 781-0125
national: (800) 736-8222
www.enterprise.com

Hertz
local: (401) 274-4043
national: (800) 654-3131
www.hertz.com

Rent-A-Wreck:
local: (401) 454-1234
national: (800) 944-7501
www.rent-a-wreck.com

Best Ways to Get Around Town

Bike

Foot

RIPTA Trolleys

Ways to Get Out of Town:

Airlines Serving Providence

Air Canada
(888) 247-2262
www.aircanada.com

American Airlines
(800) 433-7300
www.americanairlines.com

Cape Air
(800) 352-0714
www.flycapeair.com

Continental
(800) 523-3273
www.continental.com

Delta
(800) 221-1212,
www.delta-air.com

Northwest
(800) 225-2525
www.nwa.com

US Airways
(800) 428-4322
www.usairways.com

Airport

T.F. Green Airport (PVD)
(401) 737-4000

www.pvdairport.com

T.F. Green is an international airport located about nine miles from Brown and is approximately a 15-minute drive from campus.

How to Get to the Airport

The Airport Shuttle
(401) 737-2868

The shuttle runs from Brown's Faunce Arch and picks up students at 27 minutes past the hour, but you should call to confirm they are running on the day you need service.

A cab ride to the airport costs about $30.

Greyhound

Providence Greyhound Trailways Bus Terminal

1 Kennedy Plaza
Providence, RI 02903

(401) 454-0790

For schedule information, call (800) 229-9424

www.greyhound.com

The Greyhound bus service runs out of Kennedy Plaza, about a 10-minute walk down the hill from Brown.

Bonanza

The Bonanza Bus service runs out of both the bus depot off I-95 exit 25 and downtown Kennedy Plaza Bus station.

For schedule information, call (401) 751-8800.

Kennedy Plaza Bus Station

Corner of Washington and Dorrance Street, Downtown

Amtrak

Providence Amtrak Station

100 Gaspee St.
Providence, RI 02903

For ticket information, call (401) 727-7370

www.amtrak.com

Travel Agents

STA Travel

220 Thayer St.
Providence, RI 02906

(401) 331-5810

www.statravel.com

Students Speak Out On...
Transportation

> "We have free shuttles that are relatively reliable. The only problem is that there's no reason to go anywhere in the area around Brown. Getting to the train station is pretty easy, though."

Q "We're **within walking distance** to the bus or the train."

Q "Public transportation is okay. Trolleys, busses, and cabs can get you around the city. However, taxis can be late or stand you up—particularly when you really need them late at night or when you need to get to the airport or train station. Fortunately, **on a nice day, everything is in walking distance**."

Q "Public transportation is very easy. **It's everywhere**. Anything you need is a mile away, but you generally don't have to trek on foot if you don't want to. There's a trolley for 50 cents, buses, and a train station. The airport is a 15-minute drive away. There are taxis, student shuttles, and a safety walk. They've got it covered."

Q "RIPTA is hot. Rhode Island is small, so it covers the whole state. Providence is small, so you usually walk downtown (5–15 minutes) instead of taking the bus. **Getting to Boston is pretty sweet, $13 round trip and one hour each way**."

Q "Public transportation is **very easy to use**, although most students just stay on the hill."

Q "Transportation is wonderful for getting out of the city to go to New York, Boston, and Newport. **There are many trains within walking distance, and they are inexpensive as well**. Buses run in and out of the city. To tell you the truth, people rarely use them. Everyone who doesn't have a car pretty much walks everywhere. Everything in downtown Providence is pretty much within walking distance."

Q "**It's pretty good**. The commuter rail that goes to Boston is really cheap. It's great if you need to get up there during the week. I would say every couple of weeks I probably take the bus somewhere. Since Rhode Island is really small, it's really easy to get around to places, and it's pretty cheap."

Q "**Public transportation picks you up right on Thayer Street to go downtown**, and there's the campus shuttle for traveling within the Brown area. I haven't heard any complaints about either, but I'm sure there are some. Nothing's ever perfect."

Q "**You don't need a car**. Since my sophomore year, I've been working at a hospital downtown. I use the BrownMed/Downcity Express, which runs every half hour. Sometimes we have to walk home, but they might be extending the hours next year."

Q "Every other week I use the RIPTA to go visit my little sister. All you have to do is **show your Brown ID and you ride for free**. I've been doing it for a year; even though its' not official policy yet, they are changing it soon."

The College Prowler Take On...
Transportation

For such a small city, Providence offers a lot of options to travel within the city and to other big cities. If you want to get to New York or Boston, via train or bus, you can walk downhill to the station in about 10 minutes. Within the city, trolleys run to major areas of town, and they are cheap and run regularly. There are also a lot of people on campus brave enough to bring cars, so it's easy to bum rides.

Cheap and reliable, Providence's RIPTA system will get you everywhere you need without the hassle of having a car. Many Brown students use public transportation infrequently because most missions can be accomplished without having to leave College Hill, but when you need them, a trolley, bus, or train are waiting to carry you away.

The College Prowler® Grade on

Transportation: B+

A high grade for Transportation indicates that campus buses, public buses, cabs, and rental cars are readily-available and affordable. Other determining factors include proximity to an airport and the necessity of transportation.

Weather

The Lowdown On...
Weather

Average Temperature:

Fall:	54 °F
Winter:	28 °F
Spring:	47 °F
Summer:	79 °F

Average Precipitation:

Fall:	3.42 in.
Winter:	3.88 in.
Spring:	4.19 in.
Summer:	4.01 in

Students Speak Out On...
Weather

"The first years treated me well. This past year I got fed up with it. Preparing to come here, my parents bought me snow gloves and snow pants. I think I wore my snow pants once in three years."

"**Bring an umbrella; it rains a lot**. Winters are slushy. For the sunny days, the beaches at Newport are only 40 minutes away. The skating rink is downtown and great for long winter afternoons."

"**The winters are rainy**, though we get a good bit of snow on the ground from December to early February. Spring is gorgeous and summer is the typical northeast humid/hot thing from the end of June through July. Umbrellas and jackets are key; layers are important. The spring and fall sometimes feels like San Francisco with all the seasons in one day."

"The weather is what I am used to. **It snows a bit during the winter**, and it is warm and pretty during the beginning and end of the school year."

"I'm from New York, and I'll admit that **I hate Providence weather**. All of my friends from California complain about how it's not warm all the time like it is at home."

"It rains a lot because it's right near the ocean, but I really don't have any complaints. **It's livable**."

Q "The weather in Providence may **best be described as unpredictable**. It is seasonal, but we often have days of 70-degree weather followed by days of 20-degree weather. It will rain randomly and snow unexpectedly. Bring an umbrella and snow shoes."

Q "The weather is temperate. **The fall is really nice**, the winter can be hard, and spring is often late. It can be rainy, but there are some beautiful days. You'll need clothes for all seasons."

Q "It's **typical New England weather**. Winter is freezing, but otherwise, it's nice."

Q "I went to a Brown orientation in California before I came to campus freshman year. They told me the biggest problem people have is adjusting from the **lack of light during the winter**. In the winter, the sun goes down a lot earlier here."

The College Prowler Take On...
Weather

In Providence, it seems to rain two out of three days or it snows a ton. Some days in Providence are absolutely stunning, and if you visit in May, you'll probably see hundreds of students frolicking on the green. Everyone looks deliriously happy because this is one of the dozen perfect days of the year. Some winters, there are particularly heavy snow falls, which causes the school to close down for a day or two. When it's not snowing, it can be bitterly cold and depressing as the sun sets before 5 p.m. for a few months in the winter.

Most students adjust to the weather. Rain and snow-resistant clothes are a staple of every student's wardrobe. Heating in the dorms is fine, but the old houses that students inhabit off campus don't always have central heating, and gas and electricity bills run high in the cold months. While the weather is nothing to prevent anyone from coming to Brown, it is something that you must be prepared to deal with.

The College Prowler® Grade on

Weather: C

A high Weather grade designates that temperatures are mild and rarely reach extremes, the campus tends to be sunny rather than rainy, and weather is fairly consistent rather than unpredictable.

Report Card Summary

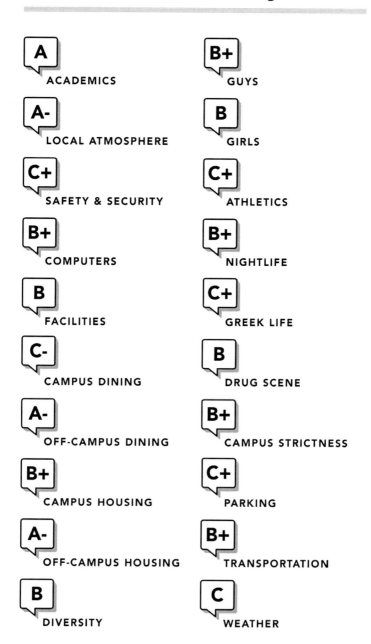

A
ACADEMICS

B+
GUYS

A-
LOCAL ATMOSPHERE

B
GIRLS

C+
SAFETY & SECURITY

C+
ATHLETICS

B+
COMPUTERS

B+
NIGHTLIFE

B
FACILITIES

C+
GREEK LIFE

C-
CAMPUS DINING

B
DRUG SCENE

A-
OFF-CAMPUS DINING

B+
CAMPUS STRICTNESS

B+
CAMPUS HOUSING

C+
PARKING

A-
OFF-CAMPUS HOUSING

B+
TRANSPORTATION

B
DIVERSITY

C
WEATHER

Overall Experience

Students Speak Out On...
Overall Experience

{ **"It was a great education. A lot of partying. I had an awesome time and wish I had made it a five- or six-year experience."**

Q "Given the choice to do it over again, I would definitely come to Brown. Before I came to college, I never thought that the size of the school would be something really important to me. Now I know I would never want to go to a school that was any bigger. **I think the size really lets you get to know a lot of people here.** All my friends who just graduated are depressed that they're leaving. I have friends at other schools who are thrilled to be getting out after four years."

Q "Brown is an Ivy League school that places more emphasis on the quality of a liberal education than on the way they are perceived by other schools. Therefore, students at Brown are generally not competitive with each other; they do not feel the need to define their credibility by their GPA. Instead, **Brown students are known for choosing to study what truly interests them**, uninfluenced by economic or social pressures."

Q "I indulged my social life and my academic life. **It was amazingly liberating**. I think I'm leaving Brown knowing who I am and where I want to go. I don't have the specific plan, but I have the ability to deal with it. I think that's pretty specific to Brown. Everyone here has a good sense of themselves. They go through their life at Brown and are comfortable with themselves after."

Q "My biggest qualm about Brown is the fact that the University doesn't have a large endowment. I know **a lot of programs are in danger of being cut**."

Q "You really make Brown what you want it to be. **There's not one social life that you have to lead**. There's not one academic life or one extracurricular life either."

Q "Before I came to Brown, I didn't think there would be a big difference between the academics, particularly advising, at the schools I was looking at. It is a big deal. **The possibilities that an open curriculum provides can be a big factor in your educational career**. Freshman year I took a lot of classes in a concentration I didn't end up pursuing. The switch wouldn't have been so easy if it wasn't for the open curriculum. It makes both the students and the professors care more. Professors know you want to be in their classes."

Q "The freedom of Brown's curriculum encourages a versatile education and **allows students to have complete discretion** when it comes to course and concentration selection."

Q "**I got tired of analyzing someone else's material** and wanted to start producing work of my own. I was tired of reading the same readings that people had been doing for a couple hundred years and writing the same papers that Brown students have been writing for decades. So, I switched concentrations and now I feel like I have a real, personal impact on the department I'm in."

Q "It's always **easy to find people who want do the same things that you want to do**. It can be aggravating how much emphasis people put on their school work, but that's to be expected. There's a broad range of people at Brown, and it's easy to find people you can connect with."

Q "Brown is awesome. **It took me a year to feel settled and good**. But since then, every year has just gotten better! Come here!"

Q "**Love it, love it, and love it**. I can't imagine myself anywhere else. The idea of graduating next year is making me incredibly upset. I really enjoyed my stay at Brown. It's been a great experience. I will treasure it forever."

Q "I hated school, but **I loved Brown**."

The College Prowler Take On...
Overall Experience

Brown has a reputation that precedes itself. As an Ivy League school, Brown carries a distinction that many students desire while knowing little about what they need or want in a liberal arts education. In that sense, Brown's liberal nature and open curriculum exceed that of the average liberal arts school. Many students redefine and rediscover themselves in college, and Brown's biggest strength is that it promotes individual development and self-discovery over the course of the undergraduate career. Internally, you have a lot of chances to make mistakes, which the University calls "discoveries," in the course of your studies. It's easy to change your concentration in the fifth, or even sixth semester.

Few people who choose Brown regret it. While it's not the school for everyone, almost anyone can find what they are looking for at Brown. Whether you are from New England or Siberia, there are clubs, organizations, classes, and fellow students who share your academic and personal interests. Most people choose Brown for its liberal nature and its strong academic resources, and few are disappointed.

The Inside Scoop

The Lowdown On...
The Inside Scoop

Brown Slang:

Know the slang, know the school. The following is a list of things you really need to know before coming to Brown. The more of these words you know, the better off you'll be.

BDH – The *Brown Daily Herald*, Brown's daily paper.

BUPD – Brown University Police Department, including everything from police reports to parking issues.

CAP – Curricular Advising Program, all first-years enter a CAP course as a way to gain exposure to academic advising at the University.

CIS – Computer and Information Services, provides e-mail, voicemail, and more.

CIT – Center for Information Technology, a landmark for directions at the center of campus and one of Brown's main computer clusters.

EMS – Emergency Medical Services, provides support for any medical emergency.

GISP – Group Independent Study Project, student-created group class.

DOC – A dean of the college.

ISP – Independent Study Project, student-created independent class.

Jo's – Nickname for Josiah's restaurant on campus.

The Gate – Pembroke on-campus restaurant that accepts meal credit.

Josiah Carberry – Mythical professor of psychoceramics.

LASO – Latin American Student Organization.

Meiklejohns – First-year peer academic councelors.

MPC – Minority Peer Councilors, one of three support counselors in first-year dorms.

OMAC – The main sports facility on campus.

OUAP – Organization of United African Peoples, umbrella organization that addresses concerns of students.

PLME – Program in Liberal Medical Education.

Randall Counselors – Academic advisors for sophomores.

R/ASC – Resource/Academic Support Center.

Ratty – The Sharpe Refractory, the main dining hall.

RC – Residential Councelor, one of three counselors in freshmen dorms.

RP – Residence Programmers, upperclassmen dorm programmers.

SAAB – Student Athletic Advisory Board.

Sci-Li – The Sciences Library.

TNT – The Next Thing, a support group for the LGBTA.

TWC & TWTP – Third World Center and Third World Transition Program.

UDC – University Disciplinary Council.

UFS – University Food Services, handles meal plan issues.

UTRA – Undergraduate Teaching and Research Assistantships, a research grant offered to students.

V-Dub – The Verney-Woolley dining hall.

WiSE – Women in Science and Engineering program.

WPC – Women Peer Counselors, one of three councelors in freshmen dorms.

Things I Wish I Knew Before Coming to Brown

- Most things can be bought at school for about the same cost as shipping, so don't be a pack rat when you are moving to campus.

- Upper-level courses are not necessarily harder than lower level ones. Don't be afraid to take harder classes as a freshman if you are interested in them.

- What you take freshman year doesn't matter, but your grades do.

- Be careful of the credit/no credit grade option. Usually, you end up getting an A anyway, or you totally slack off and get nothing out of the class.

Tips to Succeed at Brown

- Be persistent, whether dealing with classes or any other University service.

- Always seek the council of an advisor or a dean if you need questions answered or if you are having a hard time. Deans, especially, are there to protect you when things go wrong and can help improve your overall Brown experience.

- Make connections with professors or administrators who can provide good recommendations for you.

Brown Urban Legends

- Josiah Carberry is the fabled professor of psychoceramics (cracked pots) at the University. Many things around campus, such as Josiah's café and the Brown online library catalog are named after him.

- There are several secret societies at Brown.

- There is a book bound in human leather in the John Hay Special Collections Library.

- If guys step on the Pembroke seal, they will never graduate. If girls step on it, they will become pregnant.

School Spirit

School spirit at Brown is strong, but it's not necessarily reflected by the turnout at athletic events or other school functions. Although the bleachers may be empty and some people may not even know the school mascot is the Brown Bear, most people take advantage of other chances to show their school spirit. Brown students do attend political rallies, student performances, art openings, and student film screenings to support each other's work. Brown school spirit is most strongly felt in the mutual admiration among students.

Traditions

ADOCH (A Day on College Hill)

All admitted students are invited to participate in ADOCH, a two-day event in April where pre-frosh from all over the world come to check out the University and meet for the first time. While it's not required, it's the first chance for many students to meet their fellow classmates for the coming year. It's also when a lot of potential students decide to come to Brown.

The Van Winkle Gate

Every student walks through the main gates of the University exactly twice in their undergraduate career. The first week of freshman year, the gates are swung inwards toward University Hall, inviting new University members to enter the Brown campus. Years later, upon graduating, the gates are opened out, ushering the grads back into the world and ceremoniously ending their time at Brown.

The Freshman Ice Cream Social

The ice cream social on the terrace of Andrews Dorm during the first week of freshman year is a great chance for people to come out of their dorm rooms and meet other first-years.

Senior Week
The week before graduation is the last chance for seniors to celebrate before leaving the University. Underclassmen are invited to stick around in certain dorms while they work or party at the events. The week includes the campus dance, commencement ceremonies, special nights at clubs and bars, and some of the wildest parties of the year.

Spring Weekend
Usually timed to coincide with the burst of green that happens in late April, spring weekend promises a few solid rock or hip-hop shows, frat boys on couches at the greens, and people wearing smiles, shorts, and bikinis. It's a chance to cut loose before final exams.

Campus Dance
During graduation, the campus dance is a centerpiece event where graduating seniors, alumni, families, professors, and underclassmen all come together to waltz and drink on the paper-lantern lit Main Green in front of a live band.

The Gala
The spring Gala is a campus-wide event where students don their fancy rented tuxedos and escort their date to an evening of dancing in a ballroom downtown. Students rent limos or buses, dine in Providence's fanciest restaurants, and dance and party at one of Brown's biggest campus-wide student events. If you missed prom in high school, it's a great second chance.

The "Inverted Sock" Graduation Loop
Famed among University graduation processionals, the "Inverted Sock" walk down College Hill for commencement is a brilliant scheme that allows alumni, professors, and the graduating class to pass each other twice in the mile-long walk to the First Baptist Church of Providence, where the graduation ceremony occurs.

Finding a Job or Internship

The Lowdown On...
Finding a Job or Internship

Brown has the typical support to aid students looking for jobs and internships. The place to start is the Career Services Center, which offers a full range of resources to students. They have a library with walls of books for researching internships, grants, programs, and job opportunities. The staff reviews and edits resumes and cover letters and they perform mock interviews. Others include the dossier service, which keeps recommendations on file for students and a Web site that lists jobs and internships.

In the end, however, most students use Career Services sparingly and have limited results actually finding jobs through the network. Going to career services, however, can be a great way to get motivated or receive specific advice about cover letters or resumes.

Advice

There are a few good ways to get good work around the University. An easy and surefire option is to work for the University Food and Catering Service or the library system, both of which hire students for all shifts and give good hours with decent pay. For a more academic job, most professors hire students as research or administrative assistants, depending on the department. Students can get these by taking classes with the professor and demonstrating genuine interest and ability in the course, as well as developing a relationship with the professor.

Career Center Resources and Services

Career counseling interviews with Brown alumni

Job-hunting workshops

Mock Interviews

Resume building

Standardized test preparation

Firms That Most Frequently Hire Graduates

Bain and Co., Corporate Executive Board, Goldman Sachs, Google, Harvard University, Microsoft, Morgan Stanley, Peace Corps, Rhode Island Hospital, Teach for America

Alumni

The Lowdown On...
Alumni

Web Site:
www.alumni.brown.edu

Office:
Brown University
Alumni Relations
Box 1859
Providence, RI 02912
alumni_relations@brown.edu
(401) 863-7070

Services Available:
Alumni College Advising

Alumni Directory

Alumni Medical and Home Insurance

Career Networking

Maddock Alumni Center:
Located across from the Wayland Arch on campus, the alumni center offers a place for alumni functions and administrative support. The building is as a nerve center for all of Brown's alumni.

Major Alumni Events

The biggest alumni events revolve around graduation week, when alums are invited to come back to the University for a weekend to participate in class and University reunions.

Alumni Publications

BAM, Brown Alumni Magazine

BAM is published six times a year and is mailed to all alumni with active addresses.

B2B: Brown News for Brown Alumni

Sent monthly by e-mail, *B2B* offers alumni connections, campus news headlines, sports news, and other on-campus events.

Did You Know?

Famous Brown Alumni:

Todd Haynes (Class of 1985) – Writer/director

Charles Evans Hughes (Class of 1910) – Vice president, Supreme Court justice

John F. Kennedy, Jr. (Class of 1983) – Son of John F. Kennedy

Laura Linney (Class of 1986) – Academy Award nominated actress

Lisa Loeb (Class of 1990) – Singer/songwriter

John D. Rockefeller, Jr. (Class of 1897) – Son of John D. Rockefeller; philanthropist

Duncan Sheik (Class of 1992) – Singer/songwriter

Ted Turner (Class of 1960) – Media mogul

Student Organizations

Here is a list of Brown's 200+ student organizations ranging from the Art Club to the Zen Meditation Club.

Check them out at *www.brown.edu/Administration/Student_Activities/gab/index.html*

African Students Association (ASA)

African Sun

American Civil Liberties Union (ACLU)

Amnesty International

Animal Rights Coalition, Brown (BARC)

Anime Brunonia

Arab-American Anti-Discrimination Committee (AADC)

ARRR!!!

Art Forum

Asian American Student Association (AASA)

Ballroom Dance Club, Brown (BBDC)

Ballroom Dance Team (BBDT)

Band, Brown (Brown Band)

Bear Necessities, The (TBN)

Beasts of Funny

Best Buddies at Brown

Big Brothers at Brown

Bio-medical Engineering Society (BMES)

Bowling Club (College Hill)

Break Dancing Club

Brotherhood, The

Brown'sTones

Bruin Club

Bruinettes Dance Team, The Brown

Campus Alliance to End Gun Violence (CAEGV)

Cape Verdean Student Association

Catalyst, The

Catholic Pastoral Council at Brown

Celtic Cultural Organization

Chattertocks (TOCKS)

Chess Club at Brown

Chinese Students Association (CSA)

Christian Fellowship, Brown (BCF)

Clerestory

Coalition for Social Justice (CSJ)

Coalition of Bands at Brown (COBAB)

College Democrats at Brown

College Hill for Christ (CHC)

College Hill Independent (Indy)

College Republicans at Brown

Common Ground

Computer Network Management Group (CONMAG)

Concert Agency, Brown (BCA)

Concilio Latino, El

Contra and Folk Dance Society

Cooking & Baking Club

Cricket Club at Brown

Critical Review

Cultural Activities Board (CAB)

Cycling Club at Brown

Dead White Men: A Festival of Classics

Debate

Derbies, Brown

Economic Review, Brown

Enchor Singers, Brown

Engineering Society

Entrepreneurship Program

Environmental Action Network

Fantasy Gaming Society (FGS)

FBI, The

Federacion de Estudiantes Puertorriquenos, La (FEP)

Feminist Majority Leadership Alliance (FMLA)

Field Hockey Club

Filipino Alliance (FA)

Film Society, Brown (BFS)

Flying Club

Free the Children

Friends of Turkey

Fuerza Latina, La

Fusion Dance Company

Go Association, Brown

Gospel Voices of Praise

Greek Council

Green Party

Habitat for Humanity, Brown University Chapter

Harmonic Motion

Hawaii Club

Hellenic Students Association (HSA)

Hi-T

Higher Keys

Hong Kong Students Association (HKSA)

Hourglass Cafe

IMPROVidence

Independent Artist Network

International Organisation, Brown (BRIO)

International Socialist Organization (ISO)

Investment Group, Brown

Issues

Jabberwocks (WOCKS)

Japanese Cultural Association (JCA)

Jewish Student Union (JSU)

Journal of World Affairs, Brown (BJWA)

Jug, The Brown

Juggling Club, Out of Hand (OOH)

Kempo Club, Brown

Key Club, Brown

Kick Boxing Club

Korean Adoptee Mentoring Program

Korean American Students Association (KASA)

Latin American Students Organization (LASO)

Lecture Board, Brown

Lesbian, Gay, Bisexual, and Transgendered Alliance (LGBTA)

Linux Users Group, Brown (BLUG)

Lion Dance, Brown

Madrigal Singers, Brown

Mandarin Enrichment, Student Association

Movimiento Estudantil Chicano de Aztlan, El (MEChA)

Mediation Project, Brown University (BUMP)

Men's Club Soccer

Men's Club Tennis

Men's Lacrosse

Men's Ultimate Team at Brown

Merlions

MEZCLA

Mock Trial Club

Model United Nations Club

Musical Forum

Muslim Students Association, Brown (BMSA)

National Society of Black Engineers (NSBE)

Native Americans at Brown (NAB)

Next Thing, The (TNT)

Not Another Victim Anywhere (NAVA)

Nuestra Gente Mexicana

Online Gaming Society at Brown

ONYX

Organization of Multiracial and Biracial Students, Brown (BOMBS)

Organization of United African Peoples (OUAP)

Organization of Women Leaders (OWL)

Original Music Group

Orthodox Christian Fellowship

Out of Bounds

Outing Club at Brown

Oxfam at Brown

Pakistani Society at Brown (PSAB)

Photo Club at Brown

Program in Liberal Medical Education Senate Undergraduate (PLME)

American Medical Student Association Pre-Med chapter (AMSA)

Production Workshop (PW)

Reformed University Fellowship

Resumed Undergraduate Students Association (RUSA)

Shades of Brown

Shakespeare on the Green

Shotokan Karate Club, Brown University (BUSKC)

Sisters United, Brown

Snowboarding Club at Brown, the

Society for Clinical Research for Undergraduates at Brown (SCRUB)

Somos (Latino Literary Magazine)

Soul Cypher

South Asian Students Association (SASA)

Space Club at Brown

Special Events Committee (SPEC)

Spectator, Brown

Stand Up Comics, Brown

Student Labor Alliance

Student Radio, Brown (WBSR)

Students Against Acronyms

Students for AIDS Awareness

Students for a Free Tibet

Students for a Sensible Drug Policy

Students for Choice

Students for Liberty

Students for Life, Brown/RISD

Students for Responsible Investing

Students in Free Enterprise

Students of Caribbean Ancestry (SOCA)

Students on Financial Aid (SOFA)

SugarCane

Surf Club, Brown

Swing Club at Brown

Tae Kwon Do Club at Brown

Taiwan Society, Brown (BTS)

Tang Soo Do Club

Tap Club

Television, Brown (BTV)

Thai Student Association (TSA)

Tikkun Itzlach Club

Undergraduate Council of Students (UCS)

Undergraduate Council of Students Election Board

Undergraduate Finance Board (UFB)

Underground, the (UG)

UNICEF Club

Unitarian Universalist Undergrad Group

Ursa Minors

Vietnamese Student's Association (VSA)

Winebox Theatre

With One Voice

Women Students at Brown (WSaB)

Women's Club Soccer

Women's Rugby

Women's Tennis Club

Women's Ultimate

Word Performance Poetry Group

Yacht Club

Yarmulkazi! (Brown's Klezmer Band)

Young Americans for Freedom

Young Communist League (YCL)

Young Minority Investors Club

Ze French Club

Zen Community at Brown

The Best & Worst

The Ten BEST Things About Brown

1	The New Curriculum
2	The student body
3	President Ruth Simmons
4	Thayer Street
5	The College Greens
6	The restaurants off campus
7	Cheap rent
8	Close to Boston and New York City
9	Providence
10	The classes and professors

The Ten **WORST** Things About Brown

1 Eight channel, on-campus cable

2 The paltry endowment

3 Long winters

4 The meal plan

5 Providence parking laws

6 Bars close too early (2 a.m.)

7 No grocery stores within walking distance

8 Fake IDs hardly ever work

9 The stress of the housing lottery

10 Lots of rain

Visiting

The Lowdown On...
Visiting

Hotel Information:

On Campus

The Inn at Brown University
*www.brown.edu/
Administration/Conference_
Services/inn.html*
Vartan Gregorian Quad,
corner of Charlesfield and
Thayer Streets.
(401) 863-7500
Price Range: Around $100

Downtown

The Providence Biltmore
*www.providence
biltmore.com*
11 Dorrance St.
Providence, RI 02903
(401) 421-0700
Distance from Campus:
1 mile
Price Range: From $159.95

→

The Westin Providence

www.westinprovidence.com

1 West Exchange St.
Providence, RI 02903

(401) 598-8000

Distance from Campus:
1 mile

Price Range: From $239

Holiday Inn Downtown

www.holiday-inn.com

21 Atwells Ave.
Providence, RI 02903

(401) 831-3900

Distance from Campus:
1 mile

Price Range: From $107.95

Radisson Hotel Providence Harbor

www.radisson.com

220 India St.
Providence, RI 02906

(401) 272-5577

Distance from Campus:
1 mile

Price Range: From $109.95

Pawtucket (Suburb)

Comfort Inn Pawtucket

www.comfortinn.com

2 George St.
Pawtucket, RI 02860

(401) 723-6700

Distance from Campus:
4 miles

Price Range: From $90.71

Take a Campus Virtual Tour

www.brown.edu/Students/Bruin_Club/tour/corliss.html

Campus Tours

Tours are offered most days at varying times in the morning and the evening, and take about an hour. The office recommends contacting them for specific schedules.

To Schedule a Group Information Session

Call (401) 863-2378 on any weekday from 8:30 a.m.–5 p.m. eastern time for information about tours.

Interviews are recommended but not required. Off-campus interviews are offered by alumni who contact students applying for admission and arrange a time and place to meet. These interviews provide the Board of Admission with another means with which to evaluate the applicant.

Overnight Visits

A limited number of high school students can stay with current freshmen on weeknights during the semester. This is an excellent way to see firsthand the typical day of a Brown student on campus and in class. Registration is done online at the Admissions Web site.

Directions to Campus

Driving from the East

Follow I-195 West, exit at South Main Street (exit 2) and proceed to the traffic light at College Street (large courthouse at the corner).

Turn right onto College Street.

Go to the top of the hill where College Street terminates at Prospect Street, in front of Brown University's Van Winkle Gate.

Driving from the North, South, and West

Follow I-95 to I-195 East, exit at Downtown Providence (exit 1), and follow the exit ramp along the river.

At the second light (College Street), turn right.

Go to the top of the hill where College Street terminates at Prospect Street, in front of Brown University's Van Winkle Gate.

Words to Know

Academic Probation – A suspension imposed on a student if he or she fails to keep up with the school's minimum academic requirements. Those unable to improve their grades after receiving this warning can face dismissal.

Beer Pong/Beirut – A drinking game involving cups of beer arranged in a pyramid shape on each side of a table. The goal is to get a ping pong ball into one of the opponent's cups by throwing the ball or hitting it with a paddle. If the ball lands in a cup, the opponent is required to drink the beer.

Bid – An invitation from a fraternity or sorority to pledge (join) that specific house.

Blue-Light Phone – Brightly-colored phone posts with a blue light bulb on top. These phones exist for security purposes and are located at various outside locations around most campuses. In an emergency, a student can pick up one of these phones (free of charge) to connect with campus police or a security escort.

Campus Police – Police who are specifically assigned to a given institution. Campus police are typically not regular city officers; they are employed by the university in a full-time capacity.

Club Sports – A level of sports that falls somewhere between varsity and intramural. If a student is unable to commit to a varsity team but has a lot of passion for athletics, a club sport could be a better, less intense option. Even less demanding, intramural (IM) sports often involve no traveling and considerably less time.

Cocaine – An illegal drug. Also known as "coke" or "blow," cocaine often resembles a white crystalline or powdery substance. It is highly addictive and dangerous.

Common Application – An application with which students can apply to multiple schools.

Course Registration – The period of official class selection for the upcoming quarter or semester. Prior to registration, it is best to prepare several back-up courses in case a particular class becomes full. If a course is full, students can place themselves on the waitlist, although this still does not guarantee entry.

Division Athletics – Athletic classifications range from Division I to Division III. Division IA is the most competitive, while Division III is considered to be the least competitive.

Dorm – A dorm (or dormitory) is an on-campus housing facility. Dorms can provide a range of options from suite-style rooms to more communal options that include shared bathrooms. Most first-year students live in dorms. Some upperclassmen who wish to stay on campus also choose this option.

Early Action – An application option with which a student can apply to a school and receive an early acceptance response without a binding commitment. This system is becoming less and less available.

Early Decision – An application option that students should use only if they are certain they plan to attend the school in question. If a student applies using the early-decision option and is admitted, he or she is required and bound to attend that university. Admission rates are usually higher among students who apply through early decision, as the student is clearly indicating that the school is his or her first choice.

Ecstasy – An illegal drug. Also known as "E" or "X," ecstasy looks like a pill and most resembles an aspirin. Considered a party drug, ecstasy is very dangerous and can be deadly.

Ethernet – An extremely fast Internet connection available in most university-owned residence halls. To use an Ethernet connection properly, a student will need a network card and cable for his or her computer.

Fake ID – A counterfeit identification card that contains false information. Most commonly, students get fake IDs with altered birthdates so that they appear to be older than 21 (and therefore of legal drinking age). Even though it is illegal, many college students have fake IDs in hopes of purchasing alcohol or getting into bars.

Frosh – Slang for "freshman" or "freshmen."

Hazing – Initiation rituals administered by some fraternities or sororities as part of the pledging process. Many universities have outlawed hazing due to its degrading and sometimes dangerous nature.

Intramurals (IMs) – A popular, and usually free, sport league in which students create teams and compete against one another. These sports vary in competitiveness and can include a range of activities—everything from billiards to water polo. IM sports are a great way to meet people with similar interests.

Keg – Officially called a half-barrel, a keg contains roughly 200 12-ounce servings of beer.

LSD – An illegal drug. Also known as acid, this hallucinogenic drug most commonly resembles a tab of paper.

Marijuana – An illegal drug. Also known as weed or pot; along with alcohol, marijuana is one of the most commonly-found drugs on campuses across the country.

Major – The focal point of a student's college studies; a specific topic that is studied for a degree. Examples of majors include business, computer science, economics, English, history, music, and physics. Many students decide on a specific major before arriving on campus, while others are simply undecided until delcaring a major. Those who are extremely interested in two areas can also choose to double major.

Meal Block – The equivalent of one meal. Students on a meal plan usually receive a fixed number of meals per week. Each meal, or block, can be redeemed at the school's dining facilities in place of cash. Often, a student's weekly allotment of meal blocks will be forfeited if not used.

Minor – An additional focal point in a student's education. Often serving as a complement or addition to a student's main area of focus, a minor has fewer requirements and prerequisites to fulfill than a major. Minors are not required for graduation from most schools; however some students who want to explore many different interests choose to pursue both a major and a minor.

Mushrooms – An illegal drug. Also known as "shrooms," this drug resembles regular mushrooms but is extremely hallucinogenic.

Off-Campus Housing – Housing from a particular landlord or rental group that is not affiliated with the university. Depending on the college, off-campus housing can range from extremely popular to non-existent. Students who choose to live off campus are typically given more freedom, but they also have to deal with possible subletting scenarios, furniture, bills, and other issues. In addition to these factors, rental prices and distance often affect a student's decision to move off campus.

Office Hours – Time that teachers set aside for students who have questions about coursework. Office hours are a good forum for students to go over any problems and to show interest in the subject material.

Pledging – The early phase of joining a fraternity or sorority, pledging takes place after a student has gone through rush and received a bid. Pledging usually lasts between one and two semesters. Once the pledging period is complete and a particular student has done everything that is required to become a member, that student is considered a brother or sister. If a fraternity or a sorority would decide to haze a group of students, this initiation would take place during the pledging period.

Private Institution – A school that does not use tax revenue to subsidize education costs. Private schools typically cost more than public schools and are usually smaller.

Prof – Slang for "professor."

Public Institution – A school that uses tax revenue to subsidize education costs. Public schools are often a good value for in-state residents and tend to be larger than most private colleges.

Quarter System (or Trimester System) – A type of academic calendar system. In this setup, students take classes for three academic periods. The first quarter usually starts in late September or early October and concludes right before Christmas. The second quarter usually starts around early to mid–January and finishes up around March or April. The last academic quarter, or third quarter, usually starts in late March or early April and finishes up in late May or Mid-June. The fourth quarter is summer. The major difference between the quarter system and semester system is that students take more, less comprehensive courses under the quarter calendar.

RA (Resident Assistant) – A student leader who is assigned to a particular floor in a dormitory in order to help to the other students who live there. An RA's duties include ensuring student safety and providing assistance wherever possible.

Recitation – An extension of a specific course; a review session. Some classes, particularly large lectures, are supplemented with mandatory recitation sessions that provide a relatively personal class setting.

Rolling Admissions – A form of admissions. Most commonly found at public institutions, schools with this type of policy continue to accept students throughout the year until their class sizes are met. For example, some schools begin accepting students as early as December and will continue to do so until April or May.

Room and Board – This figure is typically the combined cost of a university-owned room and a meal plan.

Room Draw/Housing Lottery – A common way to pick on-campus room assignments for the following year. If a student decides to remain in university-owned housing, he or she is assigned a unique number that, along with seniority, is used to determine his or her housing for the next year.

Rush – The period in which students can meet the brothers and sisters of a particular chapter and find out if a given fraternity or sorority is right for them. Rushing a fraternity or a sorority is not a requirement at any school. The goal of rush is to give students who are serious about pledging a feel for what to expect.

Semester System – The most common type of academic calendar system at college campuses. This setup typically includes two semesters in a given school year. The fall semester starts around the end of August or early September and concludes before winter vacation. The spring semester usually starts in mid-January and ends in late April or May.

Student Center/Rec Center/Student Union – A common area on campus that often contains study areas, recreation facilities, and eateries. This building is often a good place to meet up with fellow students; depending on the school, the student center can have a huge role or a non-existent role in campus life.

Student ID – A university-issued photo ID that serves as a student's key to school-related functions. Some schools require students to show these cards in order to get into dorms, libraries, cafeterias, and other facilities. In addition to storing meal plan information, in some cases, a student ID can actually work as a debit card and allow students to purchase things from bookstores or local shops.

Suite – A type of dorm room. Unlike dorms that feature communal bathrooms shared by the entire floor, suites offer bathrooms shared only among the suite. Suite-style dorm rooms can house anywhere from two to ten students.

TA (Teacher's Assistant) – An undergraduate or grad student who helps in some manner with a specific course. In some cases, a TA will teach a class, assist a professor, grade assignments, or conduct office hours.

Undergraduate – A student in the process of studying for his or her bachelor's degree.

ABOUT THE AUTHOR

This book reflects a lot of time and effort, and I hope you find it as useful as I intend it to be. I picked up the project as a chance to reflect on my own experience at Brown, and to learn even more about the University where I spent four years of my life. Upon my graduation, I never expected to find myself writing a book the following summer.

I had a great time writing this guidebook edition to Brown, and I get a good deal of satisfaction knowing that people will know more about the University and what they can hope to find when they come to visit or to study at the school. Brown is a great place, and, like many of the students I interviewed, there's nowhere in the world I would rather call my alma mater than Brown University. If you have any questions, feel free to email me at matthewkittay@collegeprowler.com.

Matthew Kittay

California Colleges

California dreamin'?
This book is a must have for you!

CALIFORNIA COLLEGES
7¼" X 10", 762 Pages Paperback
$29.95 Retail
1-59658-501-3

Stanford, UC Berkeley, Caltech—California is home to some of America's greatest institutes of higher learning. *California Colleges* gives the lowdown on 24 of the best, side by side, in one prodigious volume.

New England Colleges

Looking for peace in the Northeast?
Pick up this regional guide to New England!

NEW ENGLAND COLLEGES
7¼" X 10", 1015 Pages Paperback
$29.95 Retail
1-59658-504-8

New England is the birthplace of many prestigious universities, and with so many to choose from, picking the right school can be a tough decision. With inside information on over 34 competive Northeastern schools, *New England Colleges* provides the same high-quality information prospective students expect from College Prowler in one all-inclusive, easy-to-use reference.

Schools of the South

Headin' down south? This book will help you find your way to the perfect school!

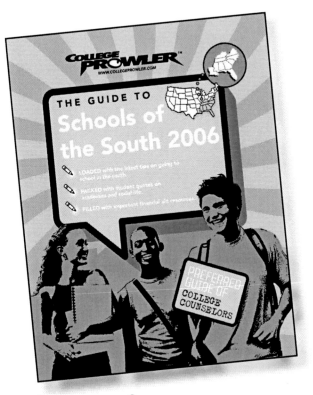

SCHOOLS OF THE SOUTH
7¼" X 10", 773 Pages Paperback
$29.95 Retail
1-59658-503-X

Southern pride is always strong. Whether it's across town or across state, many Southern students are devoted to their home sweet home. *Schools of the South* offers an honest student perspective on 36 universities available south of the Mason-Dixon.

Untangling
the Ivy League

The ultimate book for everything Ivy!

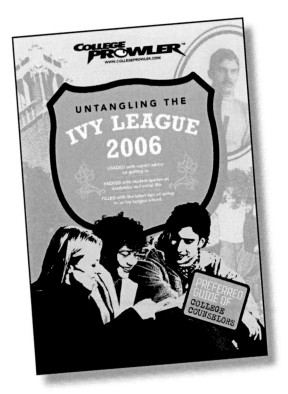

UNTANGLING THE IVY LEAGUE
7¼" X 10", 567 Pages Paperback
$24.95 Retail
1-59658-500-5

Ivy League students, alumni, admissions officers,
and other top insiders get together to tell it like it is.
Untangling the Ivy League covers every aspect—from
admissions and athletics to secret societies and urban
legends—of the nation's eight oldest, wealthiest, and
most competitive colleges and universities.

Need Help Paying For School?

Apply for our scholarship!

College Prowler awards thousands of dollars a year to students who compose the best essays. E-mail scholarship@collegeprowler.com for more information, or call 1-800-290-2682.

Apply now at **www.collegeprowler.com**

Tell Us What Life Is Really Like at Your School!

Have you ever wanted to let people know what your college is really like? Now's your chance to help millions of high school students choose the right college.

Let your voice be heard.

Check out *www.collegeprowler.com* for more info!

Need More Help?

Do you have more questions about this school?
Can't find a certain statistic? College Prowler is
here to help. We are the best source of college
information out there. We have a network
of thousands of students who can get the latest
information on any school to you ASAP.
E-mail us at info@collegeprowler.com with your
college-related questions.

E-Mail Us Your College-Related Questions!

Check out *www.collegeprowler.com* for more details.
1-800-290-2682

Write For Us!
Get published! Voice your opinion.

Writing a College Prowler guidebook is both fun and rewarding; our open-ended format allows your own creativity free reign. Our writers have been featured in national newspapers and have seen their names in bookstores across the country. Now is your chance to break into the publishing industry with one of the country's fastest-growing publishers!

Apply now at *www.collegeprowler.com*

Contact editor@collegeprowler.com or
call 1-800-290-2682 for more details.

Pros and Cons

Still can't figure out if this is the right school for you?
You've already read through this in-depth guide; why not
list the pros and cons? It will really help with narrowing down
your decision and determining whether or not
this school is right for you.

Pros	Cons
....	....
....	....
....	....
....	....
....	....
....	....
....	....
....	....
....	....
....	....
....	....
....	....
....	....

Pros and Cons

Still can't figure out if this is the right school for you?
You've already read through this in-depth guide; why not
list the pros and cons? It will really help with narrowing down
your decision and determining whether or not
this school is right for you.

Pros	**Cons**
....	....
....	....
....	....
....	....
....	....
....	....
....	....
....	....
....	....
....	....
....	....
....	....
....	....

Notes

Notes

Notes

....

....

....

....

....

....

....

....

....

....

....

....

....

Notes

....

....

....

....

....

....

....

....

....

....

....

....

....

....

Notes

....

....

....

....

....

....

....

....

....

....

....

....

....

Notes

....

....

....

....

....

....

....

....

....

....

....

....

....

....

Notes

....

....

....

....

....

....

....

....

....

....

....

....

....

Notes

....

....

....

....

....

....

....

....

....

....

....

....

....

....

Notes

....

....

....

....

....

....

....

....

....

....

....

....

....

Notes

....

....

....

....

....

....

....

....

....

....

....

....

....

....

Notes

....

....

....

....

....

....

....

....

....

....

....

....

....

Notes

....

....

....

....

....

....

....

....

....

....

....

....

....

....